PREVENTION OF CRIME AND DELINQUENCY

EUGENE DOLESCHAL

INTERNATIONAL DIALOGUE PRESS · DAVIS · CALIFORNIA

Library of Congress Card Number 83-82948
ISBN 0-89881-017-5

DEDICATED
TO MY FAVORITE
DAUGHTERS
EVE AND CLAIRE

AUTHOR

EUGENE DOLESCHAL, M.L.S., is the former director of the Information Center of the National Council on Crime and Delinquency. He is the founder of the journal *Criminal Justice Abstracts* and the author of a number of articles and books on crime, including *Toward a New Criminology, The Dangers of Criminal Justice Reform,* and *A Guide to the Literature on Organized Crime.* Currently, he is a consultant to the National Crime Prevention Council.

FOREWORD

Eugene Doleschal has performed an invaluable service for citizens concerned about crime in America. In tackling this subject — often controversial and replete with dubious claims of success — the author takes a sober and dispassionate look at a wide variety of crime prevention programs and evaluations of their success.

The reader looking for easy solutions will not be encouraged. They do not exist. Current fads are easily debunked. More complex social policy attempts to reduce crime, such as gun control legislation, are given a hard and close examination. Some conclusions are surprising. For example, the author concludes: "...the rigor and honesty with which each experiment was evaluated and the nearly unanimous negative findings leave little doubt that we do not yet know how to prevent delinquency." Such conclusions may create pessimism or even some despair among those who have devoted their careers to wrestling with these problems.

However, a complete reading will also reveal hope.

The author's brush is a broad and fast-moving one. He covers police foot patrols, neighborhood team policing, gun control, organized crime, community crime prevention, crimes against the elderly, crimes against children, and crimes against transit systems — to name a few topics.

When looking at the state of the art of delinquency prevention the author concludes that so-called "innovative" strategies merely expand current agency capacity or enhance existing services. Yet the more promising programs rest on improving conditions at the most fundamental level — the family, school, peer group, and community.

There is a growing body of literature which concentrates on the link between child abuse and neglect and later delinquent behavior. This includes physical and sexual abuse of teenagers, which often triggers them to run away. And many runaways become involved in predelinquent or delinquent activities. The author touches upon this subject, but interested readers may want to check more specialized sources in this area which explore the relationship between sexual exploitation and abuse and delinquent behavior. For example, Andrew Vachss claims that prevention of delinquency must involve intervention in early child abuse ("Child Abuse: A Ticking Bomb", *Change: A Juvenile Justice Quarterly,* vol. 5, no. 3, p. 6, 1982).

In other areas of crime prevention, there are glimmers of hope. For instance, the author reports on the existence of safe neighborhoods in the midst of turbulent communities, such as that produced by the Midwood Kings Highway program in Brooklyn, New York. Essential to the success of community crime prevention efforts are close cooperation with law enforcement and a larger community agenda: "Community crime prevention projects have greater staying power when they are part of a community effort, such as neighborhood revitalization, environmental concerns, the rehabilitation of housing, improving sanitation, resolution of tenant/landlord complaints, and the handling of citizen complaints against city government.

The author also discusses Japan, the only rapidly urbanized society where crime has decreased. This phenomenon is attributed to a homogeneous society, respect for authority, and an assumption of group responsibility. Doleschal doubts whether America will ever achieve such a dramatic reduction in crime given its heterogeneous population and lack of individual responsibility to society.

But there are concrete examples, sharing common elements, of community crime reduction in America. Success is achievable with hard work and a willingness to become involved. Citizen commitment is the key: "It is a truism that the justice system, including the police, can only react to crime, not prevent it. Collectively, citizens play the greatest role in determining how much crime there will be. The evidence suggest that there is much you and your community can do to protect against crime. The first step is to get involved.

Doleschal is right. Crime prevention is both watching out (self, property, and neighborhood protection) and helping out. "Residents who became active in crime prevention also reported feeling more responsible for their neighbors' safety and more in control of their own lives and property. "Crime prevention is also a quality of life issue. Residents who participate in community organizations often report a noticeable transformation in their quality of life. They report less fear of crime, more contact with neighbors, and increased ability to differentiate strangers from neighbors, and expanded commitment to the neighborhood, and increased willingness to intervene and report suspicious situations."

Crime prevention means caring and trust. Citizens can be effective when they act together. Experience has shown that a declining neighborhood can rebound, and that citizens who now wall themselves in with multitude locks and alarm systems could choose instead to join community life as eager participants. Crime prevention is block watch, Operation I.D., arson prevention, recreation and employment programs, and public education on child abuse and neglect. But it is also a signal that citizens have decided to regain control of their lives and their neighborhoods.

The essence of crime prevention is empowering citizens and proving that they can be effective. It is showing that they do not have to live in fear, and that they can and should help protect one another. In documenting this fact, Mr. Doleschal has done us all a great service.

John Calhoun
Executive Director
National Crime Prevention Council

CONTENTS

PART I

INTRODUCTION

CHAPTER 1

INTRODUCTION

Most Americans have definite opinions about the causes of crime and, by implication, about its prevention. Public opinion polls of the past decade have produced consistent and by now familiar findings. One in four Americans polled in one survey cited lenient laws as the cause of America's high crime rate; one in five cited drugs or drug addiction; and one in seven, lack of parental supervision, poverty, or not enough jobs.[1]

Community leaders in the *Figgie Report on the Fear of Crime* also thought they knew what causes crime. Among the factors mentioned were the failure of the criminal justice system, downfall of traditional values, unemployment, the media, population growth and mobility, drugs and alcohol, and private gun ownership.[2]

The National Urban League had specific proposals it was sure would reduce crime: full employment, decent housing, city revitalization, black economic development, adequate health care, drug treatment, handgun control, reduction in TV violence, civil rights enforcement, affirmative action, and federal aid to state and local governments.[3]

Such certainty on the part of the public and community leaders stands in stark contrast to the views of those who have devoted their careers to the study of crime and its prevention. Like Goethe's Faust, many experts confess, after years of study, that they know about as much as when they began.

Martin Gold and Hans Mattick, lifelong students of the phenomenon of juvenile delinquency, spent many years evaluating the Chicago Youth Development Project, one of the most extensive and sophisticated delinquency prevention experiments ever undertaken. Their conclusion is humbling: "After decades of effort we know almost nothing about what measures will prevent delinquency."[4]

Clifford Shaw and Henry McKay, often regarded as the "founding fathers" of the delinquency prevention movement, created the first large-scale delinquency prevention program, the Chicago Area Project (CAP). Stressing delinquency prevention through community organization, CAP sought to uplift the community by self-help from within.

In conversation with criminologist Don Sutherland, Shaw and McKay in later life revealed a deep understanding of the failure of their projects. While seeking to create a sense of community, they had ignored the social forces destroying and disorganizing that community. The businessmen who served on their boards, they said, wanted to be told that they were doing something important and that their philanthropic efforts were having the desired effect. Yet inadvertently, observed Shaw and McKay, these businessmen were causing the conditions they were trying to correct. Through the continual expansion of industry the project communities were being bulldozed apart from without while the Cap project was trying to prop them up from within.[5]

Ironically, business and industry today are blamed for abandoning the inner city, and thus for the epidemic in crime associated with the loss of jobs and decay of local neighborhoods. In fact, the relationship between crime and neighborhood deterioration is neither simple nor obvious. Studies have found that although deterioration may lead to crime in some declining areas, crime does not go down as the neighborhood is upgraded.[6]

What this suggests is that the social forces that create and maintain crime are elusive, not easily identifiable, and hard to influence. In this book we will look at a wide variety of crime prevention programs, attempting to guide the reader to "hard data" on those that have been evaluated for effectiveness. An awareness of what has and has not worked in the past will help in designing future efforts to prevent crime.

FOOTNOTES

1. Michael J. Hindelang, "Public Opinion Regarding Crime, Criminal Justice, and Related Topics," *Crime and Delinquency Literature,* 6(4), 1974, p. 522.

2. Research and Forecasts, Inc., *The Figgie Report on Fear of Crime: A Fourteen City Profile.* Willoughby, Ohio: Figgie International, Inc., 1982, 12p.

3. National Urban League, *Strategies for Controlling Crime: A Position Paper.* New York: 1978, 36p.

4. Martin Gold and Hans W. Mattick, *Experiments in the Streets: The Chicago Youth Development Project.* Ann Arbor, Mich.: University of Michigan Institute of Social Research, 1975, 354p.

5. Jon Snodgrass, "Clifford R. Shaw and Henry P. McKay: Chicago Criminologists," *British Journal of Criminology,* 16(1): 1-19, 1976.

6. U.S. National Institute of Justice, *Crime, Fear of Crime, and Deteriorization of Urban Neighborhoods,* by Richard P. Taub and others. Washington, D.C.: U.S. Government Printing Office, 1982, 60p.

CHAPTER 2

A NOTE ON THEORY

Social scientists often claim that nothing is as practical as a good theory. Theory, it is said, must guide research and action. In actual practice, however, programs are undertaken and manuals are written with no reference to their theoretical assumptions. In the literature on crime prevention there are discussions of theory and others of programs and practice, but rarely, if ever, are the two combined. Crime prevention is oriented toward a confusing array of contradictory activities.

Brantingham and Faust have proposed a conceptual model that defines three levels of crime prevention. *Primary prevention* includes those programs and techniques aimed at altering criminogenic conditions in the physical and social environment. Commercial and residential security measures and public education are examples of primary prevention. *Secondary prevention* is aimed at early identification and intervention in the lives of individuals or groups in crime-producing circumstances. This kind of crime prevention includes police patrol, diversion from the justice system, employee screening, predelinquent screening, and school intervention programs. *Tertiary prevention* attempts to prevent repeat crime through such measures as the rehabilitation of offenders, imprisonment and incapacitation, and the hiring of ex-offenders.[1]

Peter Lejins distinguishes between *prevention* and *control.* Prevention is a measure taken before a crime is committed, while control occurs after the criminal act. The distinction is important because it has implications for social action in response to crime. In crime control restricting an individual is more feasible because by committing a crime he has invited some curtailment of his rights. In prevention, compulsory public action is less acceptable. Lejins also distinguishes between punitive prevention (the deterrence of punishment), corrective prevention (removal of the causes of crime), and mechanical prevention (reduction of criminal opportunities).[2]

Others have offered their own typologies for classifying responses to crime. Elmer Johnson distinguishes a preventive ideology from the punitive and the therapeutic, subdividing the preventive type further into law enforcement efforts to deter and prevent recidivism and efforts to correct personal or social conditions that are assumed to breed crime.[3]

R.V. Clark distinguishes between "social" and "situational" crime prevention, arguing that the choices made by the typical offender favor a situational approach, one that gives more weight to the external circumstances of offending.[4]

Another theoretical model differentiates between *crime prevention* and *victimization prevention.* Cohn, Kidder, and Harvey compared members of a community organization (an example of crime prevention) to people engaged in avoidance behaviors (an example of victimization prevention). Members of the community organization reported less fear of crime and more control over crime than those who did not belong. People who depended primarily on avoidance behaviors reported more fear of and less control over crime than people who engaged in few such behaviors. In a second study, 37 women who had taken a personal defense course reported feeling more active, brave, in control, and independent, and were less worried about being home alone or out after dark. The researchers see defense training as an example of victimization prevention because it increases feelings of control and reduces fear of crime.[5]

Lavrakas and Lewis reviewed four schemes typically used to explain what people do to protect themselves against crime: (1) avoidance-mobilization activities; (2) access control, surveillance, territoriality; (3) individual-collective behaviors; and (4) public-private minded activities. In no case were these distinctions supported by empirical research; the authors propose their own classification of citizens' crime prevention behaviors and suggest how the dimensions can be measured.[6]

Finally, Gary Marx argues that theoretical approaches to crime prevention and control neglect the situation in which rule-breaking occurs. That is, the role of authorities before or during the deviant behavior which, Marx argues, is important in understanding social control as it contributes to deviance. He identifies three types of relationships between rule enforcers and rule breakers: *escalation, nonenforcement,* and *covert facilitation.* Each involves the possibility of amplifying the deviance and illustrates, from the labeling perspective, the ironic fact that authority figures often aggravate what they set out to control.[7] Of each crime prevention proposal, therefore, it must be asked what negative side-effects even a successful prevention program may produce.

The 1970s were characterized by a series of significant experiments in crime and delinquency prevention in the United States. Largely unguided by theoretical considerations, they sought to identify and test methods for reducing crime. A few were designed to empirically measure pre- and post-experimental crime and other conditions (such as fear of crime and attitudes toward police) and to document conditions during the experiment or program. Some also measured conditions in adjacent or comparable geographic areas or conditions normally projected to occur without the experiments. These were among the first large-scale, extensive crime prevention experiments to be evaluated scientifically for program outcome. The most recent and most sophisticated of these will be examined in the following chapters.

FOOTNOTES

1. Paul J. Brantingham and Frederick C. Faust, "A Conceptual Model of Crime Prevention," *Crime and Delinquency,* 22(3): 284-296, 1976.

2. Peter P. Lejins, "The Field of Prevention," in Wilyiam E. Amos and Charles F. Wellford, *Delinquency Prevention: Theory and Practice.* Englewood Cliffs, N.J.: Prentice Hall, 1967, pp. 1-21.

3. Elmer H. Johnson, *Crime, Correction, and Society.* Homewood, Ill.: Dorsey Press, 1968, 340p.

4. R.V.G. Clarke, "Situational Crime Prevention: Theory and Practice," *British Journal of Criminology,* 20(2): 136-147, 1980.

5. Ellen S. Cohn, Louise H. Kidder, and Joan Harvey, "Crime Prevention vs. Victimization Prevention," *Victimology,* 3(3/4): 285-296, 1978.

6. Paul J. Lavrakas and Don A. Lewis, "The Conceptualization and Measurement of Citizens' Crime Prevention Behaviors," *Journal of Research in Crime and Delinquency,* 17(2): 254-272, 1980.

7. Gary T. Marx, "Ironies of Social Control: Authorities as Contributors to Deviance through Escalation, Non-enforcement, and Covert Facilitation," *Social Problems,* 28(3): 221-246, 1981.

PART II

PREVENTION OF
JUVENILE DELINQUENCY

—

CHAPTER 3

STATE-OF-THE-ART OF DELINQUENCY PREVENTION

Nowhere is the failure of prevention programs and the lack of evaluation so evident as in the literature on juvenile delinquency. Both program failure and the failure to evaluate appear to derive from the lack of direction that characterizes delinquency prevention. Unlike crime prevention programs (discussed in Part III), which attempt to place physical and psychological barriers in the path of the potential offenders, the majority of delinquency prevention programs provide an array of services with only a vague and undocumented connection to the control of youthful crime.

A recent evaluation of delinquency prevention projects funded by the U.S. Office of Juvenile Justice and Delinquency Prevention (OJJDP) reflects this lack of direction. More than $20 million was expended on 16 youth programs, but a lack of clarity in OJJDP program objectives permitted grant recipients a wide latitude in the services they provided. As a result, the grantees simply continued to provide the same types of service that they had been offering for years, but now in the name of delinquency prevention. The major service provided was recreation, with the addition of some counseling, employment, education, or other assistance. Few grantees relied on even the most rudimentary screening procedures to decide which youths should receive what type of service.

The OJJDP request-for-proposals did not require, and the resulting programs did not reflect, any clear statement of the theoretical basis for delinqency prevention efforts. The programs lacked logically linked sets of objectives and activities designed to meet them. The proposals submitted by grantees envisioned a multi-service approach to counter a wide range of service deficiencies believed to contribute to delinquency, but in practice most youths received only one type of service. Services were provided to any youth within the geographic area if he or she appeared at the project site, and project resources were directed at many whose chances of becoming delinquent were not high.

Agencies varied in their organizational characteristics, but with few exceptions they offered similar programs and services. The target areas selected by most grantees could hardly be classified as communities in any manner useful for delinquency prevention. None of the grantees used community development as a primary intervention strategy, and project components were designed to expand agency capacities. The new funds were used primarily to enhance existing services.[1]

SOME THEORETICAL BASES FOR DELINQUENCY PREVENTION

Historically, the favored societal reaction to juvenile delinquency has not been prevention but control or correction of juvenile criminals or predelinquents within the juvenile justice system. With little evidence that such an approach was effective, there was a shift in philosophy in the 1960s and 1970s to a divided system of legal control for serious offenders and community service to prevent others from following this route. Prevention techniques, however, have not often been based on either good theory or good data.

A document prepared for the U.S. National Institute for Juvenile Justice on delinquency prevention argues that the most powerful theory is an integrated model combining social control and cultural deviance theories.[2] This model assumes that social processes which prevent delinquency occur in social situations (family, school, peer group, community) in the course of activities directed toward youth development. Interventions with individual delinquents have limited value since delinquency is concentrated in high-risk communities with weakened social institutions, and delinquents continue to be produced. Intervention instead should focus on changing the major socializing institutions. Special emphasis should be placed on strategies such as community organization, youth development, community committees similar to those of the Chicago Area Project, community improvement projects, parent-training, crisis intervention, surrogate families, personalized education, alternative schools, peer leadership groups, and group crisis intervention.[3]

Hawkins and Fraser have argued that delinquency prevention efforts must address delinquency's underlying causes. Their nationwide study sought to identify the theoretical prespectives of administrators of 875 delinquency prevention programs and to assess whether or not their stated views are reflected in policy and practice. The director of each program was asked to respond to 28 propositions on the causes of delinquency and methods of preventing it. The propositions served as indicators of seven major prespectives or theories including control theory, cultural deviance/differential association theories, structural/opportunity theories, labeling theory, and three general perspectives on delinquency, termed deterrence, psychological, and health/biological perspectives.

The findings suggested that practitioners are not likely to offer services that are incompatible with their views. Also, certain perspectives were associated with the provision of certain services; for example, those who subscribed to structural/opportunity theories tended to seek organizational changes that would expand opportunities for participation. However, the theoretical views of administrators did not explain much of the variation in services provided, which were determined more by the exingencies of funding and community support for particular types of service.[4]

A review of contemporary delinquency prevention strategies prepared for use by agency staffs identified five groups of prevention programs. Certain programs were judged to have no defensible basis for delinquency prevention practice, including those that explained delinquent behavior in terms of personality or biological differences and those that presumed a connection between learning disabilities and delinquency. The authors of this review suggest that, on the basis of existing evidence, psychotherapy, group counseling, and casework should not be rationalized as delinquency prevention. Nor should labeling or treatment be based on personality test scores, socioeconomic levels, intact versus broken homes, or criminal behavior.

Certain other programs represent inappropriate or ineffective uses of otherwise defensible explanations of delinquency. These include behavior modification in treatment settings, wilderness programs without follow-up, most forms of family therapy, recreation programs, employment programs that merely consume time, detached work in street gangs (which actually may increase gang activity), and increasing the punishment for offenses. Also ineffective are: admonishing young people to associate with better companions; lecturing youths on the merits of respecting parents, teachers, police, or the law; individual treatment to counter the effects of labeling; and persuading youngsters to lower their aspirations.

A third group of programs seem to have little merit, including teacher ratings to identify predelinquents, while another group offers limited benefits at substantial cost, including training parents in social learning theory and teaching work skills and middle-class behaviors to enhance the opportunities of lower-class youth.

A final group of delinquency prevention programs promises broad and lasting benefits at moderate cost, including changing school policies (such as ability grouping or tracking) that systematically rob segments of the student population of opportunities to demonstrate usefulness and competence. Also recommended are efforts to change organizational practices reflecting stereotypic presumptions about youth with certain socioeconomic, racial, or ethnic backgrounds; efforts to improve the image of law enforcement and juvenile justice; and programs designed to reduce youths' perception of powerlessness. The most fruitful arenas for delinquency prevention were identified as education, work, community service, and youthful interactions with each other and with families.[5]

But there is no proven technology of delinquency prevention. There are today many strategies in use, each oriented to some notion of the causes of delinquency and some assumptions about its prevention. A paper commissioned by the National Institute of Juvenile Justice and Delinquency Prevention describes 12 different prevention strategies:

Biological/physiological — strategies seeking to control or eliminate physiological, biological, or biopsychiatric causes of delinquency;

Psychological/mental health — strategies seeking to alter pathological mental states or the conditions believed to cause such states;

Social network development — strategies seeking to increase youths' attachments to non-deviant others;

Criminal influence reduction — strategies seeking to reduce the influence of delinquent norms;

Power enhancement — strategies seeking to increase youths' ability to control their environment;

Role development — strategies seeking to increase opportunities for youth in legitimate and personally gratifying roles;

Activity/recreation — strategies providing alternatives to delinquent activities;

Education/skill development — strategies providing youths with skills needed for nondelinquent pursuits;

Clarifying social expectations — strategies that seek to reduce inconsistent or conflicting expectations of youth;

Providing economic resources — strategies that provide resources to preclude the need for delinquency;

Deterrence — strategies that increase the costs and decrease the benefits of delinquency;

Social tolerance — strategies that seek to decrease the degree to which youths are labeled and treated as delinquent.[6]

We will turn now to some of the most recent delinquency prevention experiments that have been scientifically evaluated.

FOOTNOTES

1. National Council on Crime and Delinquency, Research Center, *The National Evaluation of Delinquency Prevention: Final Report.* San Francisco, Calif.: 1981, 541p.

2. U.S. National Institute for Juvenile Justice and Delinquency Prevention, *The Prevention of Serious Delinquency: What to Do?* by Joseph G. Weis and John Sederstrom. Washington, D.C.: U.S. Government Printing Office, 1981, 77p.

3. *Ibid.*

4. J.W. Hawkins and Mark W. Fraser, "Theory and Practice in Delinquency Prevention," *Social Work Research and Abstracts,* 17(4): 3-13, 1981.

5. U.S. Juvenile Justice and Delinquency Prevention Office, *Delinquency Prevention: Theories and Strategies,* by the Center for Action Research and Westinghouse National Issues Center. Washington, D.C.: U.S. Government Printing Office, 1979, 203p.

6. U.S. National Institute for Juvenile Justice and Delinquency Prevention, *A Typology of Cause-Focused Strategies for Delinquency Prevention,* by J. David Hawkins and others. Washington, D.C.: U.S. Government Printing Office, 1979, 43p.

CHAPTER 4

DELINQUENCY PREVENTION EXPERIMENTS

CHICAGO YOUTH DEVELOPMENT PROJECT

The Chicago Youth Development Project (CYDP), one of the best known delinquency prevention experiments, operated from 1960 to 1966 in two inner-city areas. CYDP was sponsored jointly by the Chicago Boys Club and the Institute for Social Research at the University of Michigan. It approached delinquency prevention through street-club work with youngsters and local community organization work with adults.

CYDP had the following project goals: to reduce the amount and seriousness of illegal and antisocial behavior, to help individuals meet some of their many needs, to increase opportunities for youth and help them prepare for conventional adult roles, and to promote confidence that local self-help efforts could improve the community. There were two kinds of field staff: extension workers and community service coordinators. Extension workers searched out delinquent boys to draw them into their orbit of influence, while community coordinators' organized adults in the community in the service of neighborhood youths.

For purposes of evaluation, the two experimental areas were compared with two control areas ranging in population from 18,000 to 35,000. The primary sources of information were court and police records; secondary information came from interviews with residents and executives in control and experimental areas.

According to the evaluation, CYDP was not particularly successful. It did not reduce delinquency rates among its clientele or in the target areas it served. It did not dramatically transform the lifestyles of its young clients, nor did it alter the quality of life in the inner-city areas of Chicago.

The project had some limited success with certain boys, thereby providing some guidelines for further efforts. Juvenile delinquency was reduced among boys who could be persuaded that, with the project's help, they could improve their chances of completing high school and going further. This confirmed the results of two previous efforts which effectively reduced delinquency by raising boys' optimism about their future, although neither program improved academic achievement levels. Growing optimism was the factor most predictive of the decline in delinquent behavior.[1]

Similar delinquency prevention experiments conducted in the 1960s relied on intensive social services given to boys and their families. The Seattle Atlantic Street Center experiment was the eighth such study conducted in the community among voluntary juvenile subjects. Carefully matched experimental and control groups of junior high school boys were assessed for frequency and severity of school disciplinary problems and police contacts. An evaluation of service effectiveness during the service period and for eighteen months afterward showed no positive impact. The untreated control group performed at least as well as the experimental group.[2]

A SCHOOL-BASED PROGRAM

An experiment conducted in all inner-city junior high schools in Columbus, Ohio, also was unsuccessful. A total of 1,726 (experimental, control, and comparison) seventh-grade boys nominated by their sixth-grade teachers and their elementary school principals as either headed for trouble with the law or not were followed for four years to assess the outcome of a delinquency prevention program. The preventive "medicine" consisted of the following ingredients: an all-boy seventh grade class of 25-30 meeting for three class hours in succession with the same teacher; interactional discussion interspersed with required studies; uniform presentation of material; and teachers trained to play the role of "significant others" to the boys. The theory behind the project was that the inner-city boy at the threshold of adolescence needs to internalize models of behavior and perceptions of self that can build internal self-control.

On none of the outcome variables were the experimental subjects significantly different from the controls. This was most painfully evident in school performance and in contacts with police. There were no significant differences among the groups in the number of boys who

29

had contacts with the police, the frequency of contact, or the seriousness of unreported behavior. Dropout rates, attendance, grades, and school achievement levels were similar for all three groups.

The sixth-grade teachers were not as good at predicting the boys' behavior as the investigators of the project had assumed. Personal interviews conducted two years later with experimental and control subjects also found that teachers' judgements of the outcome of treatment also were not accurate. Their belief that experimentals were much improved was not confirmed by researchers' observations. This finding underscores the need for objective evaluation based on measurable data instead of relying on the impressions and perceptions of project staff.[3]

THE ADOLESCENT DIVERSION PROJECT

A more successful, albeit more limited, experiment was conducted in Urbana-Champaign, Illinois. Designated an exemplary project by the National Institute of Law Enforcement and Criminal Justice, the Adolescent Diversion Project (ADP) exemplified the manner in which academic research can be combined with university-based services to meet a community problem. ADP was designed for groups who want to contribute to the welfare of youngsters in trouble.

In the Urbana-Champaign ADP, juveniles were taken into the program after getting into trouble that would normally lead to arrest — chronic truancy, theft, fighting, curfew violations. During the study period, 73 youths were taken into the project; 49 were assigned to an experimental group (to receive services) and 24 to a control group (no services).

ADP services were carried out by supervised university undergraduates, who spent 6-8 hours a week with their clients over a period of 18 weeks. The volunteers developed a program using either behavior contracting or child advocacy. In 1973-74 the experimental group had an average of two previous contacts with police; in the one-year period following the program they had only 0.76 contacts with police. The control group averaged 2.33 previous contacts and 1.75 contacts after one year. The 1974-75 experimental group averaged 2.21 previous contacts and 0.08 contacts after a two-month follow-up. The control group averaged 2.25 previous contacts and 0.50 juveniles were enrolled in school at time of referral to ADP. At termination, 71 percent of the experimental group and only 50 percent of the control group were still in school.

Based on the Urbana-Champaign experience, a successful ADP requires that the community be of medium size or smaller, that students deliver the services, that intervention and diversion take place early, and that university staff win the confidence of local law enforcement officials.[4]

REVIEWS OF DELINQUENCY PREVENTION PROGRAMS

A number of scholars have evaluated large numbers of delinquency prevention programs and arrived at essentially similar conclusions, namely that the vast majority of past efforts have failed. The more sophisticated the project, the less likely is success to be reported.

Dixon and Wright reviewed the literature published between 1965 and 1975 describing community-based services aimed expressly at preventing delinquency. Of 6,600 such studies, only 96 were found to contain data on project effectiveness. A subsequent review identified only ten major delinquency prevention programs that used true experimental designs.

Dixon and Wright grouped the 96 articles and reports into ten broad categories: juvenile court projects, programs using volunteers, individual and group counseling, social casework, street-corner workers, area projects and youth service bureaus, education programs, vocational programs, community programs, and a miscellaneous category. Each report was rated for internal and external validity and for policy utility. An extremely small percentage of delinquency prevention efforts had been evaluated, even minimally, and of these few showed significant results. Although many of the interventions fall into the category of tertiary prevention, the findings of this analysis are important.

There are certain types of prevention programs which have so far failed to show evidence of success. Among these are recreational programs (the service most often offered by prevention agencies across the United States), guided group interaction, social casework, and detached worker gang projects. These researchers concluded that community treatment, use of volunteers, diversion programs, youth service bureaus, and special school projects hold some promise of success. Positive results, they suggest, probably are related to the quality and quantity of services provided, but any intervention strategy will work better with some youths than with others.[5] Although Dixon and Wright believe that certain efforts show promise of success, it must be noted

31

that such optimism may not always be rewarded. For example, though Youth Service Bureaus were long regarded as a key to delinquency prevention, three evaluations of these bureaus (a nationwide evaluation, an evaluation of two Illinois YSBs, and an evaluation of a YSB in Minneapolis) showed that these programs were not serving the functions they were expected to, nor were they preventing delinquency.[6]

Lundman reviewed reports of 1,000 delinquency prevention programs, finding that only 25 actually described the nature and results of the services provided. In most cases the design of the project did not permit reliable assessment of results. For the small number of projects that could be evaluated, there were no differences in outcome between experimental and control groups. The most sophisticated and well-designed projects were reported to have failed.[7]

A more narrowly focused review of ten prevention programs using classical experimental designs came to similarly discouraging conclusions. The programs served children with propensities toward serious antisocial behavior but who participated voluntarily. The projects evaluated included: the Cambridge-Somerville Youth Study in Massachusetts, 1937-45; the New York City Youth Board Validation of Prediction Scale, 1952-57; the Maximum Benefits Project in Washington, D.C., 1954-57; the Midcity Project in Boston, 1954-57; the Youth Consultation Service in New York City, 1955-60; the Chicago Youth Development Project, 1962-68; the Seattle Atlantic Street Center Experiment in Seattle, Washington, 1962-68; the Youth Development Program in Columbus, Ohio, 1963-66; Opportunities for Youth Project in Seattle, Washington, 1964-65; and the Wincroft Youth Project in Manchester, England, 1966-68. Except for the Wincroft study, all of these experiments in delinquency prevention were deemed ineffective. The services they provided produced no better results than no intervention at all.[8]

CONCLUSION

The experiments reviewed in this chapter represent the best efforts to date to prevent delinquency. The few projects deemed successful in reducing delinquency were limited in scope (i.e. there were too few subjects to draw general conclusions) or perhaps not applicable to other locales. The rigor and honesty with which each experiment was evaluated and the nearly unanimous negative findings leave little doubt that we do not yet know how to prevent delinquency.

FOOTNOTES

1. Martin Gold and Hans W. Mattick, *Experiment in the Streets: the Chicago Youth Development Project.* Ann Arbor, Mich.: University of Michigan Institute for Social Research, 1975, 354p.

2. William C. Berleman and others, "The Delinquency Prevention Experiment of the Seattle Atlantic Street Center: a Final Evaluation," *Social Service Review,* 46(3): 323-346, 1972.

3. Walter C. Reckless and Simon Dinitz, *The Prevention of Juvenile Delinquency: an Experiment.* Columbus, Ohio: Ohio University Press, 1972, 253p.

4. U.S. National Institute of Law Enforcement and Criminal Justice, *(An Exemplary Project) Out of the Ivory Tower: a University's Approach to Delinquency Prevention.* Washington, D.C.: U.S. Government Printing Office, 1977, 28p.

5. Michael C. Dixon and William E. Wright, *Juvenile Delinquency Prevention Programs: An Evaluation of Policy Related Research on Effectiveness of Prevention Programs.* Nashville, Tenn.: Peabody College for Teachers, 1975; William E. Wright and Michael C. Dixon, "Community Prevention and Treatment of Juvenile Delinquency: a Review of Evaluation Studies," *Journal of Research in Crime and Delinquency,* 14(1): 35-67, 1977.

6. Eugene Doleschal, "The Dangers of Criminal Justice Reform," *Criminal Justice Abstracts,* 14(1), p. 143-144, 1982.

7. Richard J. Lundman and others, "Delinquency Prevention: a Description and Assessment of Projects Reported in the Professional Literature," *Crime and Delinquency,* 22(3): 297-308, 1976.

8. U.S. Juvenile Justice and Delinquency Prevention Office, *Juvenile Delinquency Prevention Experiments: a Review and Synthesis,* by William C. Berleman, National Center for the Assessment of Alternatives to Juvenile Justice Processing. Washington, D.C.: U.S. Government Printing Office, 1980, 161p.

CHAPTER 5

SCARED STRAIGHT: A CASE OF THE QUICK FIX

Since the birth of modern criminology explanations for the crime have gained popularity at certain times, soon to be replaced by other, more fashionable explanations. Lombroso popularized the idea that criminals could be distinguished from noncriminals by certain biological and hereditary traits. The positivist school of criminology changed the focus from biological causes to symptoms of social dysfunction, cultural conflict, unavailable opportunities, or poverty and slum living. Not too long ago, working mothers were regarded as a cause of juvenile delinquency, and to this day many regard learning disabilities as delinquency-producing despite evidence to the contrary.

The popularity of different cures for crime has followed similar patterns. Treatment and rehabilitation have taken myriad forms, with individual and group psychotherapy, counseling, vocational training, "intensive" community intervention, "individualized" treatment, and many other approaches being more fashionable at one time than at others. The "quick fix", or one-shot approach has at all times been seductive, whether under the rubric of treatment, prevention, rehabilitation, or deterrence. Many of these approaches have been regarded as panaceas, promoted as the all-encompassing solution to the problem. Such approaches invariably fail to live up to the unrealistic expectations held for them. Then, as their failure slowly becomes apparent, frustration sets in and the search for a new cure-all begins.

SCARED STRAIGHT

In the late 1970s a new quick fix for delinquency gained national attention and popularity. Begun by dedicated and well-meaning lifers at New Jersey's Rahway State Prison, this program was designed to turn youth away from delinquency and crime. Inmates describe the hell of imprisonment to delinquent teenagers, hoping that the three hours the juveniles spend in prison as visitors will impress them enough to prevent their return as residents. The approach is "shock-confrontation", and the style of the inmates is aggressive and dramatic, intended to show youths the most negative aspects of prison life.

In 1979 "Scared Straight", a documentary on the Juvenile Awareness program in Rahway, was aired on prime-time national television. Heralded as a breakthrough in delinquency prevention, the Scared Straight concept was implemented in various prisons around the country, claiming huge success. Scared Straight created controversy in the criminal justice system, not only because subsequent evaluations of the program did not show the 80 to 90 percent success rate claimed by the program promoters, but also because the concept was unrealistically viewed as a panacea for delinquency.

A study by researchers at Rutgers University was designed to measure subsequent delinquency of juveniles exposed to the project as compared to that of a control group. Juveniles from nine sponsoring agencies were assigned to experimental (n = 46) and control (n = 35) groups. Juvenile court records were surveyed a minimum of six months after the experimental group visited Rahway Prison and after the control group was examined for any recorded delinquent behavior. Unexpectedly, the proportion of juveniles who had no subsequent offenses was significantly higher among juveniles who *did not* attend the project (88.6 percent) than among the groups who did (58.7 percent). Of the 27 youths from both groups with prior records, 14 (51.8 percent) had no subsequent offenses. The recidivism rate of 48.2 percent for this group is not only no better than recidivism rates from other programs designed to prevent delinquency, but is worse than recidivism rates from many other programs. In the experimental group, six of the 19 youths (31.6 percent) with no prior record had subsequent records of delinquency. On a test for average seriousness of subsequent offenses, the experimental group again did significantly worse than the control group.[1]

PRISON TOURS AT MENARD

The Lifers Group at Menard Correctional Center in Illinois launched a program similar to that at Rahway. A group of inmates serving 29 years or more entered into dialogue with juveniles referred to them for an introduction to prison life. Rather than "scaring" youths straight, the Menard inmates' dialogue was graphic but honest. Prior to the dialogue juveniles were taken on a tour of the prison. A panel of five inmates spoke in turn about the monotony, trauma, and dangers of prison life. They also told how they started a life of crime and its consequences. The juveniles were then offered the opportunity to ask questions or offer comments. There was some provocation and baiting of the juveniles by inmates, but not nearly as much as depicted in "Scared Straight".

To measure the effects on juveniles of correctional center tours, six bimonthly visits to the Menard prison in 1978 were evaluated. An experimental tour group (n = 94) and a control-group (n = 67) were randomly selected from a population of adolescent males aged 13 to 18 years residing in two counties in Southern Illinois. This population was divided into youths who had been petitioned to juvenile court, youths who had been contacted by police but not referred to court, and youths who had never been contacted by police. Two personality and attitudinal tests were administered to both groups prior to and within ten days after the prison tours to determine the impact of the program on the juveniles involved.

The date showed that the tours had little positive effect and may actually have produced negative effects. The tests generally indicated no significant changes in self-concept or propensity to delinquent behavior, and when the results were analyzed for court-contacted youth only, the propensity to delinquency showed a significant increase.

A follow-up 15 months after the first tour and five months after the last showed no significant relationship between program participation and police contacts. Also, there were no significant differences in seriousness of crimes committed by experimental and control group youths following the tours. However, the experimental groups exhibited 6 percent more criminal activity after their tour than did the control group. And of the 14 youths with prior court contact who committed a crime following the tours, ten were tour group participants. It appeared that the juveniles in this group may actually have been motivated to commit crimes as a result of the tours.

Tour participants, their parents, and their teachers reported unanimous support for the program, but teachers and parents noted no major behavioral changes in youths who had participated in the tours.

The report recommended that prison tours and dialogues with inmates be discontinued. The data suggested that there may be benefits derived from the tours as part of an overall treatment program, but not as an isolated event in an adolescent's life.[2]

OTHER JUVENILE AWARENESS PROGRAMS

Michigan's Department of Correction conducted an evaluation of Project JOLT (Juvenile Offenders Learn Truth) at the State Prison of Southern Michigan (Jackson), a Scared Straight type of program. The evaluation found no benefits to juveniles from the program and the department recommended its cancellation.[3]

A Virginia Corrections Department study, on the other hand, found that the Insiders program, a juvenile awareness program run by inmates at the Virginia State Penitentiary, did contribute to a reduction in delinquency. Eighty juvenile offenders were randomly assigned to participate or not participate in the Insiders program. The frequency of intakes and severity of intake offenses of the two groups were compared six, nine, and 12 months before and after attending the program. While the groups did not differ significantly after six months, program participants had fewer intakes and less serious offenses than nonparticipants nine to 12 months after attending the program. The study suggested that a six-month follow-up period may be too short to detect program effects.[4]

A subsequent study of the Rahway Lifers Program by Sidney Langer also refuted some of the Rutgers University researchers' findings, suggesting that the program had a positive long-term effect on juvenile offenders. This study analyzed a sample of 66 juvenile offenders before and after participation in the program, finding that the experimental group's delinquent activity was relatively constant after participation, while delinquency in the control group increased substantially during the same period. Offense severity also was greater for controls than for experimentals.[5]

Adding to the contradictory findings is a study of 53 male juvenile offenders from county probation camps in California who were sent to the Squires program at San Quentin. These offenders were compared with 55 youths who did not attend the program on attitudes toward police, school, crime, prison, family, probation camp personnel, and inmates. Changes in attitude and behavior following exposure to the program were assessed by questionnaire and by a twelve-month follow-up for recidivism.

37

Youths in the experimental group showed more positive change than controls in their attitudes toward police, crime, and other criminal justice issues immediately following their visit. However, no significant differences were found between the groups 12 months after the study. The Squires program did not prevent delinquency among youths with a serious criminal record. However, lower-risk youths in the experimental group committed fewer subsequent status offenses, drug offenses, and property offenses after their visit than those in the control group. These findings were observed only for youths who were white, had six or fewer previous arrests and had committed less serious previous offenses.[6]

CONCLUSION

The National Advisory Committee for Juvenile Justice and Delinquency Prevention resolved to discourage state legislators from authorizing juvenile awareness programs on the grounds that no one has the right to intimidate children, and the American Correctional Association passed a resolution urging caution in the proliferation of programs such as the one at Rahway.[7]

Studies of the juvenile awareness program at Rahway Prison and of other programs modeled after the New Jersey program suggest that Scared Straight is not the solution to the delinquency problem. More recent programs using inmates to deter juvenile delinquency have been modified somewhat. The prison-based awareness (as opposed to aversion) promoted by these later programs does not emphasize the one-shot approach to delinquency prevention inherent in the original Scared Straight concept.

Some juvenile awareness programs do seem to prevent delinquency with some youngsters under some conditions. These programs may take a modest place in a more comprehensive arsenal of delinquency prevention strategies, but only if associated with more positive reinforcement through community or family support.

FOOTNOTES

1. James O. Finckenauer and Janet R. Storti, *Juvenile Awareness Project Help, Evaluation No. 1.* Newark, N.J.: Rutgers the State University, 1979, 27p.; James O. Finckenauer, *Juvenile Awareness Project: Evaluation No. 2.* Newark, N.J.: Rutgers the State University, 1979, 19p.

2. Greater Egypt Regional Planning and Development Commission, *Evaluation Report: Menard Correctional Center Juvenile Tours Impact Study.* Carbondale, Ill.: 1979, 123p.

3. Robert J. Homant and Gregory Osowski, "The Politics of Juvenile Awareness Programs: a Case Study of JOLT," *Criminal Justice and Behavior,* 9(1): 55-68, 1982.

4. Virginia Corrections Department, *The Insiders Juvenile Crime Prevention Program: an Assessment of a Juvenile Awareness Program.* Richmond, Va.: 1981, 58p.

5. Sidney Lagner, *Fear in the Deterrence of Delinquency: a Critical Analysis of the Rahway State Prison Lifers' Program.* Ann Arbor, Mich.: University Microfilms International, 1980, 125p.

6. California Youth Authority, *The Squires of San Quentin: an Evaluation of a Juvenile Awareness Program,* by Roy V. Lewis. Sacramento, Calif.: 1981, 162p.

7. John Blackmore, "Scared Straight: Still Needed, Still Imitated," *Corrections Magazine,* 6(2): 51-52, 1980.

PART III

PREVENTION OF CRIME

CHAPTER 6

THE POLICE IN CRIME PREVENTION

Society traditionally has looked to law enforcement to provide the first line of defense against crime. Whenever there is a real or perceived increase in crime the police often get the blame. Police departments, in turn, have relied primarily on patrol activities to prevent and deter crime.

In the 1970s several massive experiments were undertaken to analyze the effectiveness of police patrol. The experiments generally had federal funding, and several were researched by the Police Foundation with full cooperation of local departments. Routine or traditional patrol was compared to no patrol at all, preventive patrol, reactive patrol, proactive patrol, saturation patrol, location-oriented patrol (LOP), perpetrator-oriented patrol (POP), foot patrol, split-force patrol, neighborhood team policing, and field interrogation. Kansas City was the site of the first large-scale experiments in the early 1970s, followed by Nashville, Tennessee; Wilmington, Delaware; Cincinnati, Ohio; and Newark, New Jersey. The fundamental questions these experiments asked was: Can the police prevent crime? Can the police reduce crime?

THE KANSAS CITY EXPERIMENT

In 1972-73 the Kansas City, Missouri Police Department conducted an experiment to measure the effect of patrol on crime and fear of crime. Three levels of routine preventive patrol were used in the experimental areas. One area, the *reactive* patrol area, received no preventive patrol. Officers entered the area only in response to calls for help, which substantially reduced police visibility. In the *proactive* patrol area, police visibility in patrolling was increased to two to three times its usual level. In the third area, the control area, the traditional level of patrol was maintained. Effects of the three types of patrol on crime were measured by victimization rates, attitudes of the public toward police services, fear of crime, and police response time.

The experimental conditions had no significant effect on residence and non-residence burglaries, auto thefts, larcenies involving auto accessories, robberies, and vandalism — crimes traditionally considered responsive to preventive patrol. Few differences in rates of reporting crime occurred, and there were no consistent patterns.

There also were few differences and no consistent patterns in public attitudes toward law enforcement, and fear of crime was not reduced. There were no differences and no consistent patterns in the number and types of crime prevention measures used by the public. Citizens in reactive beats (perhaps contrary to expectations) tended to take fewer precautions than did citizens in proactive or traditional beats.

In general, attitudes of businessmen toward crime and police services were not affected by experimental conditions, nor was citizen satisfaction with law enforcement as a result of their encounters with police officers. Neither police response time nor citizen satisfaction with response time was affected.

In sum, the Kansas City experiment, probably the most important patrol experiment yet undertaken, revealed no important differences in level of crime, public attitudes toward police services, public fear of crime, police response time, or citizens' satisfaction with police response time.[1] The experiment set the tone for subsequent attempts to prevent crime by manipulating police patrol.

APPREHENSION-ORIENTED PATROL

Around the same time as the preventive patrol experiment, Kansas City examined another approach to reducing crime through police patrol, namely *apprehension-oriented patrol.* In August 1972, a task force of members of the tactical unit of the police department established a Criminal Information Center (CIC) and an Apprehension-Oriented Patrol Project designed to test two surveillance strategies: Location-Oriented Patrol and Perpetrator-Oriented Patrol, or LOP and POP. The CIC served the entire department as a central clearinghouse for information about criminal activity and provided support for the LOP and POP squads by identifying target locations for LOP and creating, updating, and distributing subject information for POP.

LOP involved the assignment of tactical unit officers to high-crime areas with the goal of intercepting and arresting offenders in the act of burglary and robbery. POP involved the surveillance of known criminals, again with a goal of apprehending offenders committing target crimes.

Providing information about suspects increased *regular* patrol units' arrest rates of those individuals, but made no difference in arrests by tactical units, perhaps because these officers were already acquainted with the suspects. Measured by arrest of robbery and burglary suspects, LOP was slightly superior to POP. LOP produced more target-crime arrests per officer-hour expended, with a greater percentage of arrests resulting in criminal charges.

LOP was superior to both POP and regular patrol in effectiveness on most of the important criteria: arrest productivity, effectiveness in disposition of arrests, removal (of suspects) effectiveness, and officer-citizen conflict. POP was superior to regular patrol on most of the criteria.

Although LOP produced more officer-citizen conflict, it expended fewer officer-hours per target arrests, fewer officer-hours per charge filed as target crime, and fewer officer-hours per conviction for target crimes than either POP or regular patrol.

Despite their positive findings, particularly for LOP, the evaluators concluded that neither of the surveillance strategies was substantially more effective than the traditional mix of tactical unit activities in the Kansas City Police Department. The experiment was judged expensive; specialized apprehensive activities divert resources from regular police functions and incur extraordinary expenses for equipment such as special detection devices and rental cars. In addition, both LOP and POP produced a substantial increase in citizen complaints. The experiment hinted at a common trade-off in crime prevention: In the face of an intensified law enforcement effort, a decrease in fear of crime may be associated with an increase in resentment of police intervention in citizens' lives.

PATROL EXPERIMENTS IN NASHVILLE

Nashville, Tennessee was the site of another attempt to determine whether "saturation patrol" would prevent crime. Four high crime zones in metropolitan Nashville were chosen for the study. Two zones were subjected to saturation patrolling over a ten-day period from 9 a.m. to 5 p.m., while the other two received saturation patrol from 7 p.m. to 3 a.m. Overall patrol movement was increased to four times normal levels. Four tactical squad cars, plus the car regularly assigned to the zone, were on patrol during the experimental period. In addition, slow patrol movement under 20 miles per hour was increased to around thirty times normal levels.

Effectiveness of saturation patrol was measured by comparing rates of Part I crime during a 30-day pre-experimental period, the ten-day experimental period, and a post-intervention period. A multiple-baseline design and time-series analysis showed statistically reliable changes in reported crime (particularly robbery, burglary, and aggravated assault) during both night patrols, but not during the day patrols. In the day-patrol zones crime remained unchanged while the night zone showed a significant decrease. After the ten-day experiment was terminated there were statistically reliable increases in the two night-patrol zones to the level slightly higher than before the experiment began. There were no significant changes in the day-patrol zones.

In no adjacent zone was there a significant change in the level of Part I reported crime during the experimental period, showing that crime was not simply displaced when patrol was increased in the target areas. Similarly, there was no apparent change in crime reports within the experimental zones during shifts when saturation patrol was not in effect. The increase in crime in night-patrol zones following the experiment suggested that displacement may have been temporal rather than geographical. Apparently, once potential offenders perceived the experiment of saturation patrol to have ended they increased their criminal activities to make up for lost time.

As in Kansas City's LOP and POP experiment, the researchers concluded that no matter how many crimes were suppressed during the experiment, the Nashville Police Department could not afford to maintain patrol at the saturation level.[3]

A second Nashville experiment examined the effects of police saturation patrolling strategies on burglary rates. Three zones with a serious residential burglary problem were chosen as the target areas. Thirty-five men from various branches of the police department were selected to form a specialized burglary foot patrol. During saturation patrol, eight to 15 men patrolled each of the three target areas during the 8 a.m. to 4 p.m. shift over a five-week period. Information was analyzed on home burglary rates for the three shifts in the target areas and for three randomly chosen comparison areas.

For all three target zones, the foot patrol failed to decrease burglary substantially. A time-series analysis showed no significant changes in the level of burglaries during the experiment. The home burglary rates in the experiment areas for other shifts also showed no significant changes, and there were no significant changes in three control zones. Specialized burglary foot patrol did not serve its intended purpose of reducing burglary in the experimental areas, lending support to the conclusion of the Kansas City experiments that variations of common patrol strategies have little, if any, effect on crime.[4]

TESTING THE SPLIT FORCE

Another variation of police patrol is the *split-force patrol,* in which call-for-service and crime-prevention functions are assigned to different groups within the patrol force. The Wilmington, Delaware, Bureau of Police participated in a split-force experiment from December 1975 through November 1976. To implement the concept, the Bureau had to increase the efficiency of its call-for-service response force (the basic patrol force) so that a prevention patrol force (the structured patrol force) could be formed.

During the experiment Wilmington's crime rate per 100,000 population decreased by 6.1 percent, but the city's overall clearance rate for both violent and property crimes dropped significantly. The structured patrol force increased clearances (+105.5 percent) by the patrol division at the expense of the detective division, whose own clearances dropped dramatically (−61.4 percent), causing an overall decrease in the departmental clearance rate (−28.0 percent). The increase in patrol division clearances was attributed to the immediate follow-up by structured-patrol officers investigating felony incidents, but conflict between officers and detectives led to an overall decrease in clearances.

While officials of the Wilmington police department, including the chief, were pleased with the split-force program, only one-third of the rank-and-file officers wanted the experiment continued. Although they regarded the approach as effective, they did not like the divisiveness it engendered, the lack of sector identity, and the boredom with fixed-post assignments. The public perceived no differences in service quality due to the experiment

The Wilmington experiment illustrates a finding common to police efforts to reduce crime, namely the phenomenon of mixed results. The Wilmington crime rate did decrease, but crime in that city had been fluctuating over the preceding seven years. The structured patrol force increased its clearance rate, but there was an overall decrease in the department's clearance rate. Police officials were pleased with the experiment and wanted to continue, but rank-and-file officers were two to one against it, and the public was indifferent.[5]

NEIGHBORHOOD TEAM POLICING

In neighborhood team policing the delivery of police services is decentralized; a team of police officers assumes responsibility for crime control and law enforcement within a given area. One of the most significant experiments in neighborhood team policing was conducted in Cincinnati. Cincinnati's Community Sector Team Policing, or COMSEC, was designed to improve police-community relations and reduce crime. District I of Cincinnati was selected as the experimental area because of its diverse neighborhoods and its high crime level. One of the ingredients of the experimental program was foot patrol.

Police department crime reports and household and commercial victimization surveys showed that COMSEC was more successful than traditional policing in reducing burglary. Reported residential burglary in District I declined more than the established trend for that area. The proportion for small businesses struck by burglary and robbery decreased significantly in District I but not elsewhere. Small businesses in the district reported to police a larger percentage of crimes than they had before COMSEC, a sign of greater confidence in and satisfaction with law enforcement. Both robbery and burglary of neighborhood businesses in District I declined during the first 18 months of program operation, although they returned to pre-COMSEC levels during the last 12 months when the program began to deteriorate and morale among officers began to fall.

A major accomplishment of the program was its effect on fear of crime. Fewer citizens in District I felt "very unsafe" walking in their neighborhoods at night and most believed that officers were more likely to arrive when called. Both citizens and businessmen in the district noticed more frequent use of foot patrol, and more of them recognized the officers who worked in their neighborhoods. Police officers also reported positive changes in the breadth of their jobs, in their independence, and in their influence over decisions, although most of the reported gain in job breadth was lost by 18 months. Satisfaction with work showed a similar pattern.

48

The one clearly successful result of neighborhood team policing, a reduction in fear of crime, was observed in several subsequent experiments in which the visibility of police on foot patrol was the chief ingredient.[6]

One disturbing aspect of crime in Cincinnati during the experiment was that reports of burglaries outside the experimental zone increased significantly, in sharp contrast to the steady decline evident before team policing in the experimental area was begun.[7] Did COMSEC merely displace burglary from the experimental district to other areas of the city? The data strongly suggest that it did.

OTHER PATROL EXPERIMENTS

An experiment in the San Diego Police Department sought to determine whether improved and increased field interrogation (FI) would reduce crime. Police officers were given extensive training in recognizing valid FI situations and in conducting interrogations.

Three patrol areas were chosen for comparison, matched on demographic and socioeconomic composition and prior reported crime histories: a control area, where FI activities were conducted as usual; a special FI area, where interrogations were conducted only by officers given special supplemental FI training; and no-FI area, where interrogations were suspended entirely for the nine-month study period. FI policies were evaluated in terms of effects on reported crimes considered suppressible through patrol activities; total arrest rates; and police-community relations.

Specialized field interrogation did not result in lower crime rates. The monthly frequencies of suppressible crimes did not change significantly in either the control area, where interrogations were conducted in the traditional manner, or the special FI area. However, the experiment provided law enforcement with an important finding: Some level of FI activity, as opposed to none, does deter suppressible crimes. In the no-FI area the monthly frequency of suppressible crimes increased during the experiment, then decreased when interrogations were resumed. Monthly averages of suppressible crime went from 75 before the experiment to 104 when interrogations were suspended and back to 81 when interrogations were resumed. Monthly frequencies of total arrests in all study areas were not significantly influenced by the levels of FI activities, nor were police-community relations.[8]

Albuquerque, New Mexico, was the site of yet another attempt to determine whether the deployment of a special police unit using alternating modes of marked and unmarked patrol to saturate high-crime areas would decrease property crime in those areas. Again, the results were negative. Property crime rates and residential burglary in particular, were not reduced by marked or unmarked units patrolling the areas, or by the use of both as a team. It was concluded that increasing police activity in order to prevent crime was not warranted.[9]

THE RETURN TO FOOT PATROL

Most American police departments abolished foot patrols in the 1930s and 1940s in favor of patrol cars equipped with radios. In the past few years, however, with public pressure on governments and law enforcement to "do something" about crime, walking patrols have made a comeback. The trend is nationwide, and it is affecting even cities and towns where foot patrol has hardly been used in the past.[10]

To learn more about a strategy that police officials and citizens often cite as an effective means of controlling crime the Police Foundation evaluated the use of foot patrol in 28 cities in New Jersey. The foot patrol experiment in Newark was given special attention. Eight beats patrolled on foot consistently since the beginning of the Safe and Clean Neighborhood Program were matched in four sets of two beats each, based on the number of residential and non-residential units found on each beat. Of each pair of beats, one was randomly assigned to continue foot patrol, while in the other the practice was discontinued. In addition, foot patrol was instituted in four areas where it had not been used before. The effects of foot patrol were evaluated on five measures; reported crime, arrests, victimization surveys, fear of crime, and satisfaction with the police among residents and businessmen.

The first significant finding was that residents were fully aware of foot patrol. Although only vaguely aware of police car patrol and not particularly sensitive to team policing, the public is keenly aware of the presence of policemen walking their beats. Crime levels, as measured by victimization surveys and reported crime, were not affected for the general public or for business establishments. Foot-patrol officers had little mobility, did not answer many calls for services, and made fewer arrests than their more mobile counterparts in squad cars. Nonetheless, residents in areas where foot patrol was added were more convinced that crime was decreasing than were residents of other areas.

50

Street disorders, serious crime, drug use, vandalism, victimization of the elderly, and car theft were all perceived as less of a problem, although objective measures of victimization and reported crime confirmed none of these perceptions. Residents' perceived level of safety in the beats with new foot patrol increased in eight of the nine measures used.

The findings were thus strikingly similar to the Cincinnati experiment. While foot patrol does not affect crime, it does affect citizens' fear of crime, the protective measures they take to avoid crime, and the perceived safety of their neighborhoods. When foot patrol is added, citizens' fear of typical street crime goes down and generalized feelings of personal safety go up. Foot patrol therefore has striking, positive side-benefits. Citizens become less fearful and are more willing to use the streets. Foot patrol, the Police Foundation study found, also fosters personal contact between citizens and police that elevates the opinion of each toward the other — no small feat in some Newark neighborhoods. The study also found that police officers patrolling on foot are exposed to rich new sources of information about crime.[11]

CONCLUSION

The experiments reported in this chapter, and many lesser ones not as rigorously evaluated, yield some information about the effectiveness of police in controlling crime. The most optimistic conclusion that can be drawn is that in itself police patrol on foot or in cars may produce a reduction in particular types of crime, at least for short periods of time. This can be accomplished by substantial increases in patrol or the introduction of patrol to an area where none existed before. Specialized police tactics may have a marginal effect on crime, and upgrading the status of a given task may improve police performance, although again only for short periods of time. Such strategies are invariably accompanied by high costs; sometimes by public resentment of police or rivalry between different groups of police officers.

The various new ways of organizing patrol, often calling for more focused patrol tactics, offer no conclusive proof of greater effectiveness. A National Institute of Law Enforcement and Criminal Justice report on traditional preventive patrol concludes that there are no accurate measures of the effect of patrol in non-experimental situations and that routine patrol can be altered considerably without affecting crime patterns.[12]

Another study concluded that a strategy aimed at direct deterrence is effective only when the blocking of opportunity is sufficient to cause competition between the demand for crime opportunities and the opportunities remaining unblocked. Police patrol as practiced by most departments achieves little deterrence, and the increase caused by doubling or tripling the patrol force may be insignificant. It is possible for a patrol force to provide saturation coverage in certain areas at certain times at great financial cost, but police prevent more crime by general deterrence than by direct deterrence.[13]

Reviewing the impact of neighborhood team policing in 18 American cities, the National Institute observed that the results were inconclusive. Reported crime in some cities improved relative to control areas while in others there was no difference. Because of the contradictory evidence and methodological problems of some of the studies it is impossible to assess the effect of team policing on crime rates.[14]

The following are some consistent findings from the major experiments discussed in this chapter:

Saturation patrol and other intensive patrols are extremely costly to police departments, more costly in fact than the value lost by victims of crimes suppressed.

In many instances there is a problem of either geographic or temporal *displacement;* i.e., criminals operate in nearby non-experimental areas, they wait for a costly experiment to end, or they operate during non-experimental police shifts.

The ideal crime prevention program should cause crimes reported to police to *increase* (due to increased public confidence in law enforcement) while actual victimizations should *decrease.*

Intensified patrol procedures may produce more police-citizen conflict and more complaints against the police. A reduction in fear of crime may be accompanied by an increase in fear of law enforcement, particularly in minority neighborhoods.

Certain isolated (as opposed to consistent) differences in experimental conditions may be due to a random occurrence, rather than to any crime prevention efforts.

A consistent bright spot is the positive effect of police officers on foot patrol. Although they may not reduce reported crime or victimizations, they dramatically affect citizen perceptions of crime. Citizens consistently report less fear of crime, greater feelings of safety, improved attitudes toward police, and increased mobility in their neighborhoods. If a major goal of crime prevention is an improvement in the general quality of life, then foot patrol may be the most important ingredient.

Can the police do better in preventing crime when citizens cooperate in community crime prevention programs? We will turn to that subject next.

FOOTNOTES

1. Police Foundation. *The Kansas City Preventive Patrol Experiment,* by George C. Kelling and others. Washington, D.C.: 1974, 59p.

2. Midwest Research Institute; Police Foundation, *Three Approaches to Criminal Apprehension in Kansas City: an Evaluative Report,* Tony Pate, Robert A. Bowers, and Ron Parks. Washington, D.C.: 1976, 124p.

3. John F. Schnelle, "Patrol Evaluation Research: A Multiple-Baseline Analysis of Saturation Patrolling During Day and Night Hours," *Journal of Applied Behavior Analysis,* 10(1): 147-154, 1977.

4. John F. Schnelle and others, "Social Evaluation Research: The Evaluation of Two Patrolling Strategies," *Journal of Applied Behavior Analysis,* 8(4): 353-365, 1975.

5. Public Systems Evaluation, Inc., *An Alternative Approach in Police Patrol: The Wilmington Split-force Experiment,* Cambridge, Mass.: 1977, v.p.

6. Urban Institute, *The Cincinnati Team Policing Experiment: A Summary Report,* by Alfred I. Schwartz and Sumner N. Clarren. Washington, D.C.: Police Foundation, 1977, 63p.

7. *Ibid.,* p. 27.

8. Systems Development Corporation, *San Diego Field Interrogation: Final Report,* by John Boydston. Washington, D.C.: Police Foundation, 1975, v.p.

9. William F. Wagner, *An Evaluation of a Police Patrol Experiment,* Ann Arbor, Mich.: University Microfilms, 1978, 109p.

10. Mary Jo Patterson. "They're Walking the Beat Again," *Police Magazine,* 5(4): 53-60, 1982.

11. Police Foundation, *The Newark Foot Patrol Experiment,* Washington, D.C.: 1981, 137p.

12. U.S. National Institute of Law Enforcement and Criminal Justice, *National Evaluation Program Phase I Summary Report: Traditional Preventive Patrol,* by Theodore H. Schell and others. Washington, D.C.: U.S. Government Printing Office, 1976, 91p.

13. Lucius J. Riccio, "Direct Deterrence — an Analysis of the Effectiveness of Police Patrol and Other Crime Prevention Technologies," *Journal of Criminal Justice,* 2(3): 207-217, 1974.

14. U.S. National Institute of Law Enforcement and Criminal Justice, *National Evaluation Program Phase I Summary Report: Neighborhood Team Policing,* by William G. Gay and others. Washington, D.C.: 1977, 45p.

CHAPTER 7

COMMUNITY CRIME PREVENTION

Law enforcement resources in most industrialized nations have not increased in proportion to the growth in demands for protection, so existing resources are under increasing pressure and police have had to persuade citizens to do more for themselves. It is clear, at any rate, that crime prevention cannot be accomplished by the police alone. Unless citizens report crimes promptly, unless they come forward with information to help make arrests, unless they are willing to be witnesses in court, and unless they participate, individually and collectively, in crime prevention efforts, crime will not be perceived to be under control.

Yet citizen actions often falter. The Census Bureau's annual victimization surveys show that only one-third of all serious crimes are reported to the police. Even when people do report crimes, they tend to delay before calling the police. A Kansas City response-time analysis revealed that the average citizen waits so long to report a crime that police, no matter how fast they respond, have little chance of making an arrest on the scene. Where the witness to a crime is so indecisive in reporting it, efforts to reduce police response time probably would be useless.[1]

In the courts, too, criminal cases often wash out because witnesses fail to cooperate. A District of Columbia study found that half of all arrests end in dismissal, most often because of problems with a witness. Community crime prevention programs find it difficult to maintain citizen participation, and many such programs are short-lived.[2]

Law enforcement, it has been argued, should be a negotiated contract between the public and the police; both must acknowledge their mutual responsibility. The police must do what they can to put back into the hands of citizens the social problems of their communities. Communities, in turn, must recognize that crime control is not the sole province of the police.[3]

Financial support for community crime prevention programs has come from federal, state, and local governments and from non-governmental sources such as local banks, businesses, and service organizations that have been willing to give small grants to underwrite neighborhood crime prevention activities. Some programs involve only a small number of residents who have joined hands to protect their immediate neighborhood or building, while others have involved thousands of citizens to protect a large geographical area. The initiative sometimes has come from police departments, which have sponsored such programs as Operation Identification (in which valuables are engraved with numbers), security surveys and target-hardening of residences and businesses, or neighborhood block watches. However, many police departments treat crime prevention as a secondary public relations activity, and the initiative for action has had to come from small groups of concerned citizens or local civic organizations. Nationally, association such as the Jaycees, Kiwanis Clubs, and the General Federation of Women's Clubs have started programs and have urged their members to participate.

Among the most popular community crime prevention programs are those designed to reduce crime opportunity. Operation Identification encourages citizens to mark their personal property for easy identification in case of theft. Security surveys are conducted to recommend improvements to homeowners and tenants so they can protect themselves against burglary. Some programs provide burglar alarms and security locks to needy residents. Citizen car patrols and block-watchers programs, which are among the most popular, seek to alert citizens to suspicious behavior and to report their observations to police. Crime opportunity can also be reduced through environmental design, the topic of Chapter 10.

Community crime prevention programs are sometimes designed to improve the work of the criminal justice system. For example, some projects monitor police response time, file citizen complaints against police departments, and make demands for better service. Court-watching programs, in which citizens monitor court proceedings, represent another effort to improve the justice system's responsiveness. Projects also may aid and counsel victims or assist witnesses with court procedures.

The most effective programs have targeted their efforts to deal with specific community problems or have combined various standard program elements in a comprehensive project with heavy citizen involvement.

CRIME WATCH

During the 1970s hundreds of community crime prevention programs were funded by federal and state agencies, and by 1977 seventeen states had established statewide crime prevention programs, generally designated "Crime Watch".

A proposed model crime watch program consists of three phases, to be implemented successively until all are operating simultaneously. In the first phase, focused on residential security, citizens are instructed how to make their homes less inviting targets for burglars and other intruders. Elements of this phase include security techniques, citizen watches, and Operation Identification. The second phase, focused on commercial security, assists businesses in securing themselves against burglary, robbery, bad checks, credit card fraud, and employee theft. The third phase, focused on personal security, emphasizes measures that citizens can take to reduce their chances of becoming a victim of crime.[4]

The case studies of one state's Crime Watch program provided an early record of experience with this type of program. The statewide program sponsored by the Minnesota Governor's Commission on Crime Prevention and Control focused on mechanical methods of crime prevention — placing obstacles in the path of the would-be criminal to make the commission of crime more difficult. The program included home burglary prevention, Operation Identification, commercial and personal security, theft and fraud protection, and techniques to control rural crime and organized crime. More than 260 police and sheriff's departments, serving 95 percent of the state's population, participated in the program. Consistent with the results in other jurisdictions, the rate of burglaries for residences participating in Minnesota Crime Watch was substantially less than for the community as a whole.[5] However, data on program activity collected at statewide and local levels were inadequate to measure overall program effectiveness. The Minnesota program may not have reduced crime in the state or in entire communities, but individual participants reaped the benefits of reduced victimization.

CITIZEN PATROLS

One of the most popular means of involving citizens in community crime prevention are citizen patrols. Their effectiveness in reducing crime has not been fully evaluated, but an exploratory study conducted by Rand Corporation examined 109 residential patrols in 17 urban areas in the United States.[7] At the time of the study (1976) it was estimated that between 800 and 900 citizen security patrols were operating in the United States.

The Rand study divided resident patrols into four types: building, neighborhood, social service, and community protection patrols. Building patrols were found to be effective in preventing crime, but for the other types effectiveness was difficult to measure. Resident patrols are occasionally susceptible to vigilantism, with neighborhood patrols more inclined to such behavior than building patrols. The Rand study recommends that if resident patrols are used, they should be instructed to report incidents to police, but not to intervene, unless the patrol members are professional guards.

A Citizen Crime Reporting Project established in Columbus, Ohio, was designed to discourage potential offenders by having citizens patrol on foot in designated areas. Patrollers also reported crimes in progress and gathered information about criminal incidents for use by the police department in investigation, apprehension, and conviction. At the time it was evaluated, the program was contributing to a reduction in the crimes of burglary and auto theft within the project area and there was overwhelming support for the project by residents.[8]

COMMUNITY ORGANIZATION

An example of a project with rather ambiguous results was the Minneapolis Crime Prevention Demonstration. The project was designed to limit criminal opportunities by reshaping the social and physical environment in three Minneapolis neighborhoods. Block clubs and business associations were formed for most of the blocks in two of the neighborhoods, and about half the blocks in the third neighborhood had at least one crime prevention meeting. However, although crime went down in at least two project neighborhoods (it increased in the third) the evaluation did not indicate that the project itself was responsible. The results of the Minneapolis program were thus equivocal at best.[9]

A successful experience with community organization is provided by the Community Congress of San Diego, which in 1978 was awarded a grant to organize residents to reduce crime. Program elements included neighborhood watch groups, neighborhood anti-crime committees, youth planning councils, a citizen-police family services protective team, and bicycle and property identification programs. All activities were designed to use as many teams of volunteers as possible. Although there were no comparisons with control communities, the neighborhoods in which block watch programs were conducted did experience a decrease in four crime categories most common in those neighborhoods: residential theft, petty theft, auto theft, and vandalism. Even more important were the intangible benefits of improved living conditions and more positive feelings among residents. The program significantly increased communication among neighbors, and residents viewed their neighborhoods as safer and expressed less fear of crime. The researchers observed that neighborhood crime reduction can be enhanced by organizing residents around issues other than crime.[10]

Another program in San Diego involved the police and sheriff's departments in community crime prevention activities. Interaction between citizens and police at neighborhood watch meetings had several positive consequences. Those who attended meetings were likely to engage in practical preventive measures such as improving home security, engraving valuables with a driver's license number, and placing neighborhood watch stickers in windows. Residents who became active in crime prevention also reported feeling more reponsible for their neighbors' safety and more in control of their own lives and property.[11]

Neighborhood associations in St. Louis, Mo., were found to be effective in reducing crime: Those studied were responsible for a 10 to 15 percent reduction in property crimes and a 15 to 25 percent reduction in violent crime.[12]

HARDENING THE TARGET

Many communities in the United States have implemented target-hardening or opportunity-reduction techniques to reduce burglaries city-wide. One of the best examples is Atlanta's Target Hardening Opportunity Reduction (THOR) project, aimed at that city's burglary and robbery problem. THOR included the following elements: security surveys (pointing out actions a citizen or business can take to enhance physical security); Operation Identification; an emergency contact system (contacting business owners in the event of a burglary); organizational involvement (presentations to civic, social, and business groups); and research projects. Comparisons of reported crime before and after program implementation showed reductions of 13.7 percent for burglary and 22.1 percent for robbery. There were bigger drops for businesses than for residences. Commercial burglary decreased 12.7 percent and commercial robbery 41.7 percent. Residential burglary was reduced 14.1 percent, but residential robbery increased by 17.2 percent. Security surveys were identified as the single more important element in the success of the program.[13]

Security surveys seek to recognize, appraise, and reduce losses by analyzing physical facilities, including homes and commerical establishments, and recommending improvements in security. The premises are inspected, the owner is advised of security weaknesses and methods to overcome them, and later contacts are made to check on implementation of recommendations. Effects on crime may then be evaluated. In 1976 the National Institute of Law Enforcement and Criminal Justice identified more than 300 survey-performing agencies, and observed from the data available that victimization does seem to be lessened when survey recommendations are implemented.[14]

Operation Identification (OI) is designed to reduce the incidence of burglary by encouraging citizens to engrave an identifying mark on their personal property as a deterrent to theft and an aid to recovery. The assumption is that if an item is readily identifiable, a new element of risk is added to the disposal of stolen goods, thereby discouraging burglaries and theft. OI was established statewide in Illinois and an evaluation was conducted to determine whether it was capable of reducing theft. Official criminal statistics and census data were used to trace trends over time in participating and non-participating communities, supplemented by some hypothetical performance measures. With crime statistics refined to the most detailed level (e.g. residential burglaries committed in day-light hours in which identifiable property was stolen), the evaluation found that Operation Identification, as implemented in Illinois, did not reduce criminal activity statewide.[15]

A nationwide review of Operation Identification projects found that most have been unable to recruit more than a handful of participants in their target areas (only ten of 65 responding projects indicated that they had enrolled more than 10 percent of their target households), and recruitment costs per participant are quite high. Project participants do have significantly lower burglary rates after joining: There were burglary decreases for program participants of 33 percent in Seattle, 25 percent in St. Louis, 19 percent in Phoenix, and 7 percent in Denver. Confirming the findings of the Illinois evaluation, OI projects have not been associated with reductions in city-wide burglary rates. No evidence was found that OI produces an increase in arrests or convictions of burglars. The presence of identification markings does not significantly reduce opportunities to dispose of stolen goods or increase their

60

recovery and return, and burglars are not reluctant to victimize an OI household or to steal marked property. The significant burglary reductions for OI participants may be primarily due to non-OI causes, such as the tendency of participants to employ other target-hardening techniques. Engraving a mark on personal property apparently is not enough.[16]

Some of the burglaries that were prevented by OI households may be displaced to the households of non-participants. An evaluation of the Seattle OI project failed to detect any significant level of displacement, either to other crimes or to non-participating households, but studies in Denver and St. Louis suggest some displacement to neighboring areas. It is not known whether OI is capable of reducing buglaries community-wide or city-wide, but one crime prevention model postulates that 90 percent of community residents would have to be enrolled before city-wide crime prevention is observed.[17]

Displacement also occurred in connection with a neighborhood target-hardening program in Kalamazoo, Michigan. Volunteers patrolled the neighborhood during the evening hours and distributed crime prevention literature during a ten-month period in 1977. Compared with the year before the project was initiated, burglaries decreased by 26 percent primarily because of improvements made in home security and the guarding of property against theft. Burglars were 38 percent less successful in their burglary attempts, and there was a 51 percent reduction in the monetary value of goods stolen. However, there was a 57 percent increase in the incidence of burglaries on adjacent streets during the ten months, a classic example of crime displacement.[18]

TWO SUCCESSFUL PROGRAMS

Seattle's Community Crime Prevention Program (CCPP) was part of a comprehensive burglary reduction plan that in 1977 earned LEAA's designation as an exemplary project. Using a combination of prevention programs to deter crime, it includes Operation Identification, neighborhood watches, target hardening, and volunteer community organizers. The goal of CCPP is to help residents recognize their vulnerability to burglary and to learn how to reduce risks through cooperative action.[19]

Evaluation of the program showed that it realized the ideal outcome: an increase in rates of reporting burglaries from 51 to 76 percent combined with a reduction in burglaries of participating households of from 48 to 61 percent. A higher proportion of burglary-in-progress calls was made to police during the program than before the program began. During 1977 CCPP served approximately 5,280 households per year at an annual project cost of $46.14 per household. Much of this cost should be considered recovered through the savings associated with a reduction in burglary. There was no evidence of displacement of crime to non-participating neighborhoods.[20] The Seattle program provides solid evidence that, while crime rates may not be reducible on national, state, or even city-wide levels, a comprehensive program well planned and implemented can reduce victimization among program participants.

A second success story comes from North Asylum Hill in Hartford, Connecticut, where architects, residents, and police have cooperated in a comprehensive program that includes team policing. Two studies of this important project detail the promise and the pitfalls of neighborhood crime prevention.[21]

The Hartford project was designed to reduce residential burglary and street robbery and fear of these crimes in a neighborhood showing physical and social deteriorization and a rising crime rate. The program combined changes in the physical characteristics of the nighborhood with police and resident activities in an effort to increase resident control and reduce opportunities for crime.

The program had several components. By closing some streets and making others one-way, through traffic using residential streets was substantially reduced. In addition, the residential character of the neighborhood was reinforced by creating visual entrances to the neighborhood from the busy streets surrounding it. A neighborhood police team also was created, and a Police Advisory Committee was developed to strengthen ties between police and residents. Formal organizations in the neighborhood were created or strengthened to provide a means for residents to work on neighborhood problems. Rather than affect crime and fear directly, these several components were intended to create an environment in which residents could effect the rate of stranger-to-stranger crime and fear of crime.

An evaluation conducted after one year of program operation drew data from victimization counts taken before (in 1973, 1975, and 1976) and after (1977) the program was in effect; police data for 1973-76; police officer questionnaires completed before and after program implementation; and vehicular and pedestrian traffic counts on key streets before and after street changes were implemented. Two types of analysis were made: comparison of burglary and robbery rates in North Asylum Hill before and after program implementation, and comparison of these crime rates with those in several control areas and in the city of Hartford as a whole.[22]

Victimization survey results showed a 42 percent reduction in burglaries in the target area between 1976 (before program implementation) and 1977 (after implementation), reversing a trend of increasing burglary. The rate dropped from 18.4 per 100 households in 1976 to 10.6 in 1977. There was a parallel (33 percent) decrease in fear of burglary in the target area following program implementation, again reversing a pattern of increasing fear. Target-area and control-area burglary rate patterns were markedly different following program implementation, although the patterns had been similar in all areas before the program began. There was no evidence of displacement of burglary from North Asylum Hill to adjacent areas.

Victimization survey results also showed a 27.5 percent decline in robbery in the experimental area between 1976 and 1977, from 5.1 to 3.7 per 100 persons, reversing a trend of increasing robbery. There was a parallel reduction (24 percent) in fear of robbery in North Asylum Hill. The reduction of target-area robbery following program implementation was in contrast with the control-area pattern of continued increase. There was a significant increase in the rate of robbery in one control area immediately adjacent to North Asylum Hill in 1977 — a possible case of crime displacement. Arrests for burglary and robbery in North Asylum Hill rose markedly.

The comprehensiveness and interlocking organization of the crime prevention program apparently contributed to the initial success of the Hartford experiment. Increased resident involvement in and responsibility for the neighborhood was identified as the most important reason for the success in crime reduction. Police team members became more positive in their perceptions of the neighborhood as a place to live, of the willingness of residents to assist the police, and of resident input in police operations.

A second evaluation of the Hartford program was carried out in 1979, three years after implementation.[23] By this time the program had changed, in large part because of a marked reduction in manpower of the Hartford Police Department. One result of that reduction was that arrests for burglaries and robberies in Asylum Hill dropped sharply to near pre-program levels. However, the community organizations were still active and the traffic through the area, if anything, was even lower than in 1977.

The most important finding of the second evaluation was the degree to which community residents had changed their behavior and attitudes toward informal control of their neighborhood. They reported increased use of the neighborhood, a better ability to recognize strangers, a much higher incidence of intervening in suspicious situations, and a markedly increased perception of neighbors as a resource against crime. Every measure related to informal social control improved, but burglary and robbery increased between 1977 and 1979, returning to levels that could have been predicted from city-wide trends. The rise apparently was related to the reduction in police manpower.

The Hartford experiment nevertheless demonstrated that environmental changes can strengthen a neighborhood, and that strengthening informal social control can have a positive effect on fear of crime. Aggressive, effective arrest activity that has the support and cooperation of residents can deter crime in a neighborhood.

PLANNING COMMUNITY CRIME PREVENTION PROGRAMS

Written for planners, community organizers, and members of neighborhood groups involved in crime prevention, a report by the Minnesota Crime Prevention Center identifies more than 400 programs operating nationwide in 1980 and offers the following observations. Planning for crime prevention generally does not follow textbook planning precedures. Official agencies use formal planning techniques more often than do citizens' groups, but the latter usually handle community politics better. Most crime prevention projects experience conflict over one or more aspects of the program. Representation is an issue common to all projects, but few projects are representative of all interests. Citizens can be motivated to initiate community crime prevention programs, but few programs relying solely on volunteers persist over a long period. Police support and cooperation are crucial to the success of a community crime prevention program.[24]

A guide issued by the National Crime Prevention Institute of the University of Louisville stresses that, at the start, community crime prevention programs should not attempt to prevent all crimes for all groups in all places. There should be action priorities reflecting a reasonable mix of the crime problems themselves, the concerns of citizens, and available resources. Impact must be assessed in terms of what can reasonably be expected from particular program strategies, not that which might be hoped for over the life of the program. Crime prevention will fail almost be definition if they are forced to prove their overall worth during any given time interval. The crime prevention program must be judged on a strategy-by-strategy, year-by-year basis. If crime prevention works at all, it works in the most specific crime-target situation possible, and it is only by gradually building a wider and wider circle of effective strategies that crime prevention achieves a community-wide impact.[25]

CONCLUSION

Citizens themselves, not the police or the government, are primarily responsible for the security of their neighborhoods. The police play a critical role, and government support is necessary, but citizens must begin to take direct action against crime. Lavrakas maintains that multipurpose voluntary associations at the neighborhood level should be the primary vehicles for community crime prevention. Prevention programs, he suggests, will have some elements in common, but different communities will devise their own approaches to controlling crime.[26]

The following ingredients for success in a community crime prevention program can be identified from the programs described in this chapter:

Community crime prevention must have the support and guidance of local police. Police must provide the leadership and stimulate citizen commitment. Aggressive, effective arrest activity in support of citizen volunteer crime prevention activity is a key ingredient of a successful program.

Community crime prevention must be an integrated, comprehensive effort. Isolated crime prevention tactics such as Operation Identification or Crime Watch alone are not enough.

A comprehensive community program should include some or all of the following elements: security surveys, target hardening, Operation Identification, Crime Watch, neighborhood patrols, neighborhood associations, and an emergency contact system.

In some projects displacement of crime away from target areas was observed. This phenomenon must be dealth with in crime prevention programs if one neighborhood is not to achieve crime reduction at the expense of another.

65

Evaulation of experimental programs has shown that crime generally is not reduced throughout an entire state or city. Several programs, however, have reduced victimization in target neighborhoods or among participating residences.

Residents who participate in community organizations often report a noticeable transformation in the quality of their lives. They report less fear of crime, more contact with neighbors, an increased ability to differentiate strangers from residents, an expanded commitment to the neighborhood, an increased willingness to intervene in and report suspicious situations, a feeling of control over their lives and property, and a greater satisfaction with the police.

Community crime prevention projects have greater staying power when they are part of a larger community effort such as neighborhood revitalization, environmental concerns, the rehabilitation of housing, improvement of sanitation, resolution of tenant-landlord conflicts, and the handling of citizen complaints against city government.

FOOTNOTES

1. Kansas City (Missouri) Police Department, *Response Time Analysis.* Kansas City: 1977, 63p.

2. U.S. National Institute of Law Enforcement and Criminal Justice, *Community Crime Prevention.* Washington, D.C.: U.S. Government Printing Office, 1977, 18p.

3. Colin Moore and John Brown, *Community Versus Crime.* London: Bedford Square Press, 1981, 150p.

4. John DeCicco, "Crime Watch: Implementation of Statewide Crime Prevention Programs," *Criminal Justice Quarterly,* 5(3): 56-66, 1977.

5. U.S. General Accounting Office, *Report on Administration of the Program to Reduce Crime in Minnesota.* Washington, D.C.: 1974, 54p.

6. Minnesota Governor's Commission on Crime Prevention and Control, *Minnesota Crime Watch: the Law Enforcement Crime Prevention Program.* St. Paul, Minn.: 1974, 45p.

7. Rand Corporation, *Patrolling the Neighborhood Beat: Residents and Residential Security.* Santa Monica, Calif.: 1976, 154p.

8. Edward J. Latessa and Harry E. Allen, "Using Citizens to Prevent Crime: An Example of Deterrence and Community Involvement," *Journal of Police Science and Administration,* 8(1): 69-74, 1970.

9. Minnesota Crime Control Planning Board, *Evaluation of the Minneapolis Community Crime Prevention Demonstration.* St. Paul, Minn.: 1979, 253p.

10. Community Congress of San Diego, *Evaluation and Final Report: Community Anti-crime Consortium.* San Diego, Calif.: 1980, v.p.

11. San Diego Region Comprehensive Planning Organization, *Community Crime Prevention: What Works?* San Diego: 1979, 16p.

12. C.W. Kohfeld and others, "Neighborhood Association and Urban Crime," *Journal of Community Action,* 1(2): 37-44, 1981.

13. Touche Ross & Co., *City of Atlanta Bureau of Police Services: Target Hardening Opportunity Reduction Project (THOR),* Atlanta, Ga.: 1976, 144p., app.

14. U.S. National Institute of Law Enforcement and Criminal Justice , *Crime Prevention Security Surveys.* Washington, D.C.: U.S. Government Printing Office, 1976, 32p.

15. Hans W. Mattick and others, *An Evaluation of Operation Identification as Implemented in Illinois.* Chicago: University of Illinois at Chicago Circle, Center for Research in Criminal Justice, 1974, 240p., app.

16. U.S. National Institute of Law Enforcement and Criminal Justice. *National Evaluation Program Phase I Summary Report: Operation Identification Projects: Assessment of Effectiveness.* Washington, D.C.: 1975 28p.

17. *Ibid.*

18. Paul H. Selden, *Using a Neighborhood Crime Prevention Program to Reduce Residential Breaking and Entering.* Ann Arbor, Mich.: University of Microfilms, 1978, 121p.

19. U.S. National Institute of Law Enforcement and Criminal Justice, *An Exemplary Project: Community Crime Prevention,* by Paul Cirel and others. Washington, D.C.: U.S. Government Printing Office, 1977, 166p.

20. *Ibid.*

21 Hartford Institute of Criminal and Social Justice, *Reducing Residential Crime and Fear: The Hartford Neighborhood Crime Prevention Program,* by Brian L. Hollander and Linda R. Brown. Hartford, Conn.: 1978, 71p.; U.S. National Institute of Justice, *Neighborhood Crime, Fear, and Social Control: A Second Look at the Hartford Program.* Washington, D.C.: U.S. Government Printing Office, 1982, 183p.

22. Hartford Institute, *ibid.*

23. National Institute of Justice, *supra* note 21.

24. Minnesota Crime Prevention Center, *Planning Crime Prevention Program,* by Marlys McPherson and Glenn Silloway. Minneapolis: 1980, v.p.

25. University of Louisville, National Crime Prevention Institute, *The Practice of Crime Prevention (Volume I): Understanding Crime Prevention.* Lexington, Ky.: 1978, v.p.

26. Paul J. Lavrakas, *Citizen Self-help and Neighborhood Crime Prevention.* Evanston, Ill.: Northwestern University Center for Urban Affairs and Policy Research, 1982, 44p.

CHAPTER 8

PLANNING CRIME PREVENTION: THREE CASE STUDIES

A PLANNING MODEL

One of the most useful documents for planning community crime prevention happens to be a brief report produced by the British Home Office, whose Working Group on Crime Prevention concluded that crime prevention needed to be tackled more systematically.[1] This group proposed a new approach to the planning of prevention efforts, one that may be applied in many different types of community and to many different kinds of crime.

First the situation in which a particular type of crime occurs — say, theft from supermarkets — is thoroughly studied to determine what conditions are necessary for the offense to be committed. Then the various barriers to fulfillment of each of these conditions are identified and the practicability, likely effectiveness, and costs of each are estimated. The most promising measures that inhibit commission of the crime then are selected.

A study was undertaken to test the usefulness of this planning model in practice, using school vandalism in an urban area as the crime problem. In the first stage of the study government officials, local police, and other interested parties were consulted and vandalism records were examined to find schools suitable for participation in the project. The research team adapted the analysis of school vandalism to take into account local circumstances and prepared a dossier for each participating school, including an analysis of its problems and an assessment of possible remedies.

Measures recommended for the schools included the following. At five schools, what initially appeared to be vandalism was found to be, for the most part, accidental breakage from ball games. The use of hardened glass to replace broken windows was recommended. At four schools, vandalism, although not severe, consisted of damage to windows, sanitary fittings, fences, and roofs. The main recommendations were a mixture of target-hardening measures. At one school with a moderately severe problem of vandalism and break-ins where school grounds were open to children during non-school hours, it was recommended that a park warden be employed. For a school with a severe problem of vandalism and break-ins the following recommendations were made: fence off part of the school grounds as a play area, close the rest of the school grounds to the public, and erect a caretaker's bungalow on the site. For the interim, it was recommended that a security guard be hired.

This systematic approach to crime prevention planning encouraged a more coherent and informed response to the crime problem. It not only produced better recommendations for preventive measures, but it did so in part by discouraging the use of inefficient measures rather than the adoption of new ones. The approach did have some weaknesses, however. It did not encourage innovation to the extent that the Working Group had hoped; most preventive measures recommended were physical changes to harden the target rather than social measures to reduce motivation for crime. Some planning steps, especially the initial offense analysis, were quite time-consuming, and the tasks of maintaining liaison with the groups involved and monitoring the implementation of recommendations were costly in their use of staff resources.

Little was learned about youth who vandalized schools, but considerable knowledge was gained about the offense itself. That much of the cost of repairs arose from accidental damage suggests that a narrow concentration on vandalism may not be cost-effective. Most of the measures implemented were target-hardening devices, and it is reasonable to expect that those directed toward accidental damage were likely to be effective against this kind of loss.

CRIME PREVENTION PLANNING IN BROOKLYN

The British Home Office approach to crime prevention planning seems best suited to the small community or the community with a small and defined crime problem such as vandalism. The approach will be much less effective in a complex urban environment characterized by a multiplicity of crime problems, escalating crime rates, and deteriorating neighborhoods.

One of the finest examples of crime prevention planning in such an environment is presented by the Midwood Kings Highway Development

Corporation (MKDC), a massive, sophisticated, comprehensive crime prevention effort in Brooklyn, New York. MKDC was a spectacular success in developing broad-based citizen participation in crime prevention, in linking crime prevention with neighborhood revitalization, and in developing cooperative relationships with police and other city government officials. The experience of the Midwood Kings Highway Development Corporation demonstrated the value of taking a comprehensive approach to reclaiming neighborhoods plagued by crime and deteriorization. It deserves closer examination as one of the country's best examples of such an effort.

The MKDC is a neighborhood revitalization project which battles to save its community on three fronts. First, through its efforts to organize the community, thousands of Midwood residents have joined citizen car patrols, block-watching programs, and other anti-crime efforts. Secondly, the corporation operates as an informal "town hall" for Midwood citizens, giving the community a strong voice for lodging complaints and demanding services from police and other government officials. Third, the corporation has been successful in obtaining federal, state, and city funds for rehabilitation of housing, revitalization of businesses, youth recreation, education, and environmental projects.

Midwood consists of a 200-square block area in central Brooklyn. Its 64,000 residents are mainly middle-income, with a high proportion of senior citizens. About 80 percent of the community is filled with one- or two-family homes, but about 70 percent of the population lives in apartment dwellings. Until the recent past Midwood was a middle-class neighborhood, but before MKDC was formed it experienced an influx of poor and transient residents, rising crime rates, and deteriorization of its commercial and apartment buildings. The safety and desirability of the community declined, and by 1976 citizens perceived their neighborhood to be at a dangerous point.

In response to these trends, the local Community Planning Board requested volunteers to serve on committees that would identify neighborhood needs. Ten committees were formed, devoted to such problems as housing, recreation, crime prevention, education, fundraising, sanitation, youth, and senior citizens. Committee members were recruited for their experience with these problems. The Housing Committee, for example, included landlords, homeowners, and those who worked with the local housing agency. Some committees obtained assistance from the New York City Planning Department and interested faculty members from nearby Brooklyn College.

Each committee was mandated to conduct a needs assessment and formulate recommendations. The Housing Committee, for example, determined that the future of Midwood depended on improvements in the quality and appearance of housing. In recommending improvements, it targeted housing on busy streets that were highly visible to neighbors and visitors. The Recreation Committee found that local parks were unused and in deplorable condition and targeted one park for immediate upgrading. The New York Sanitation Department was pressured to remove litter, money was raised for park beautification, and a local school horticulture department was persuaded to tend the plants. Once the park was improved it was again frequented by residents, thereby creating demand for additional improvements.

MKDC was incorporated as a nonprofit, state-chartered organization. Its planning board looked for activists with a long record of service in the community to serve on the board of directors. About 40 Midwood residents, mostly professionals and businessmen, were recruited.

Before 1976 Midwood residents were becoming increasingly concerned with the area's rising crime rate. In 1979 the Midwood area ranked third highest in New York City in residential burglary and first in both auto theft and larceny from autos. A survey conducted soon after MKDC was formed revealed that many residents were moving or planning to move from the area because of the crime problem. The police department was greatly handicapped because of a series of manpower reductions, which had cut police manpower by one-third. The police department attempted to launch various community crime prevention programs, but efforts were scattered and uncoordinated. Similarly, some citizen groups in Midwood were involved in crime prevention, but lacked coordination and widespread support from the community.

A grant proposal submitted to the federal Office of Community Anti-Crime Programs was drafted by members of MKDC with assistance from local civic groups, the borough president, representative Elizabeth Holtzman, the New York City Police Department, police captains from the three precincts of the Midwood area, and other governmental officials. The authors of the proposal examined the area's crime problem, crime prevention progams implemented by police and homeowner's groups, and needed improvements in these programs to increase their effectiveness in reducing crime.

MKDC defined seven goals for the crime prevention project. In order of priority they were: to gain the support and participation of large numbers of local residents; to reduce rates of three target crimes — burglary, auto theft, and grand larceny from automobiles; to reduce fear of crime, instilling in residents the belief that the crime problem in Midwood was serious, but controllable; to provide residents with a place for lodging complaints about the local criminal justice system; to gain police cooperation and support of community crime prevention efforts, to integrate the anti-crime project with other projects aimed at community stabilization and improvement; and to provide technical assistance to nearby communities interested in mounting similar crime prevention projects.

The MKDC project was designed to expand, organize, and facilitate the operation of existing community crime prevention activities, most of which were handicapped by a lack of coordination and low levels of community interest and participation.

The project had seven major anti-crime components: *resident organizing,* including civic, block, and tenant organizing and block watchers; *patrols,* including civilian car patrols, moped patrols, and tenant patrols; *property protection,* including home security surveys, Operation Identification, and automobile decals; *equipment distribution,* including intruder alarms, whistle and shriek alarms, and door locks for the elderly; *public education,* including a crime prevention newsletter and crime prevention education; *youth services,* including youth recreation and a "Helping Hands" program; and *criminal justice system support,* including court watchers and legislative surveillance. The array of measures appeared sufficient to make criminals in Midwood intensely uncomfortable.

On June 1, 1978, MKDC received its first grant from the Law Enforcement Assistance Administration (LEAA). Paid staff members were recruited, screened, interviewed, and hired by the board of directors. The original staff was composed of an executive director, a project director, an assistant director, a community organizer, a security specialist, and a youth recreation coordinator. Initial staff efforts were concentrated on publicizing the project, developing relationships with local groups, and recruiting Midwood residents as volunteers. Above all, input from local police in planning crime prevention activities was solicited.

Within one year, MKDC was able to achieve all objectives stated in the grant proposal (e.g., form 50 block associations, establish a car patrol base) and was awarded a second grant by the Office of Community Crime Prevention. The MKDC obtained additional funds from a variety of federal, state, city and private sources. Since its inception in 1978 to the end of 1982 MKDC has received about $900,000 in direct grant awards and has channeled over $12 million into building improvements throughout the Midwood community.

MKDC's major policies are determined by a 40-member board of directors that meets as a group once a month. The board represents a wide range of interests, including civic associations, school boards, and parent associations. All board members reside in Midwood and serve MKDC as volunteers. The corporation employs 12 full-time staff members, seven of whom are assigned to projects, including the anti-crime project. In addition to its directors, the anti-crime project employs a security specialist, who assists in all phases of project activity, and a youth recreation coordinator, who oversees the youth recreation component.

In screening applicants for MKDC staff positions, three requirements were established: residence in Midwood; a history of community involvement; and flexibility in work hours. MKDC sought staff with relevant vocational backgrounds. For example, the original project director was a former police detective; the anti-crime project director has a background in retail security and is a member of the auxiliary police. MKDC's security specialist was also a retired police detective with experience in organizing car patrols. It was felt that a good relationship with police would be easier to establish if a staff member had a law enforcement background.

The crime prevention project of MKDC includes most of the standard crime prevention activities found in similar projects throughout the United States, but two features make it unique. The first is the remarkable high number of residents who have volunteered their services; the project boasts 40,000 volunteers, nearly two-thirds of the area's total population. MKDC has emerged as the hub of an effective communications network for Midwood and has given it a unified, strong voice that gets the attention of government. The second unique feature of the Midwood anti-crime project is its integration with other projects directed at housing, commercial revitalization, and the environment. The anti-crime project was the first to receive funding and its success provided impetus for the implementation of other projects. The anti-crime project mobilized the community, generating interest in the corporation and encouraging residents to volunteer.

Cooperation between citizens and the police is considered the cornerstone of the anti-crime program. Police-community relations had reached a low point before MKDC was established. Residents saw the police as a part of the problem, while the police complained of a lack of citizen cooperation. The MKDC project turned the situation around. Police input was solicited in the early stages of planning so that the project would not be seen as competing with the police department. Selection of a former police detective as the first project director helped to foster supportive police-community relations. And police fears were reduced by continuing efforts to assure them that the work of the volunteers would not be used to justify further cutbacks in police personnel within the project area.

Police have cited several ways in which MKDC has had a positive effect on police-community relations: Midwood residents are seen as good complainants against criminal defendants and reliable witnesses, being highly motivated and cooperative during criminal investigations and proceedings. MKDC uses its organization to recruit large numbers of residents for the court-watchers program. Arresting officers sometimes receive letters of commendation from the MKDC project director. When known habitual criminals are back on the street, citizens often report this to MKDC, which in turn informs the precincts. Neighborhood associations sometimes raise funds for special police needs such as bulletproof vests and patrol cars. Complaints about police services are often made to MKDC, which then calls its contacts at precinct headquarters, giving the police a chance to work out problems with people they know.

In organizing Midwood residents MKDC established or reorganized existing civic, block, and tenant associations, block watchers, civilian car patrols, moped patrols, and tenant patrols. When the project first began, staff members divided the area into six sections, and neighborhoods and buildings with the worst crime problems were targeted for the first organizing activities. This stands in contrast to many other crime prevention projects which initiate their programs in areas with less severe crime problems to help establish their reputations.

Initial contacts with residents aimed at publicizing MKDC's activities and encouraging participation were achieved through a newsletter and presentations by MKDC staff at association meetings. MKDC staff also canvassed blocks and apartment buildings, with the community organizer going door-to-door to talk with residents. Asking about problems in their neighborhoods and about their interest in forming block or tenant groups. Once a resident expressed a willingness to host a meeting, MKDC helped to schedule it and prepared publicity flyers for distribution to neighbors.

In anticipation of the meeting, the community organizer developed a list of problems mentioned by residents during initial contacts. While security and crime problems were high on the agenda, other problems were noted as well, such as poor sanitation, elevator malfunctioning, or landlord-tenant disputes. The broad focus on neighborhood conditions was deemed important, because improved physical and social conditions serve to heighten citizens' sense of control over their environment.

The project's original objective of organizing at least 50 block and tenant associations during the first year was easily met. By September 1980 over 200 block and tenant associations were organized, all of them incorporated in their local civic organizations. MKDC's direct involvement in fledgling block and tenant associations does not go beyond the initial organizing meeting, and it becomes the responsibility of the block steering committee to sustain resident interest in crime prevention. The success of the anti-crime activities in Midwood is attributed in part to the large number of senior citizen volunteers, whose flexible schedules allow them to engage in volunteer activities during working hours.

Each of the 235 block and tenant associations in Midwood now has an operating block-watchers network. At meetings, MKDC stresses the "every-citizen-a-block-watcher" concept and the responsibility of all neighbors to be alert, to help each other, and to report suspicious activity to police. At the end of block meetings copies of the police department training manual for this program are distributed.

In conjunction with the block-watch program, MKDC introduces the idea of a telephone alert chain. Civic associations distribute to each block and tenant association member a card to affix by the telephone containing the names and phone numbers of three neighbors. This enables an entire block or apartment building to be alerted to an emergency within a few minutes. Participants are instructed to dial 911 to report the emergency to the police, turn on outside lights at night, and, if they wish, respond to the scene of the emergency with at least three other neighbors.

Before the LEAA grant award, two of the civic associations in Midwood had purchased cars and citizen-band radio equipment and were operating their own civilian car patrols four nights a week.

MKDC's project goals were to add three new patrol cars, enlist 500 additional patrol volunteers, expand the patrols to canvass the entire Midwood project area, and coordinate all patrols through a central communications center. Residents expressed a great deal of interest in volunteering for car patrols, which were viewed by them as visible proof of their own determination to protect and revitalize their neighborhoods. By 1980 over 1,500 citizens had become patrol volunteers.

Three-hour training classes for new patrol volunteers are conducted by the anti-crime project director and security specialist in conjunction with police trainers. The principal themes emphasized during these classes are: patrollers should never get out of the patrol car; the base operator should be obeyed; the car should be "respected;" and patrollers should cooperate with the public. Patrollers are told to drive at a speed of 10 miles per hour, instructed in the use of the CB radio, and given police department documents explaining regulations governing civilian car patrols.

Two problems anticipated by MKDC concerning civilian car patrols were vigilantism and boredom. Vigilantism is largely avoided by the screening of patrol volunteers, though a patroller occassionally must be dismissed because of inappropriate behavior. Participant boredom is avoided by assigning patrollers responsibilities that are not strictly related to crime prevention but are of benefit to the community. Patrollers take note of neighborhood conditions, watching for potholes, broken street lights, poor sanitation, and non-functioning traffic lights. Patrols are periodically checked by MKDC's security specialist to ensure that proper precedures are followed.

Because manpower reductions severely restricted police patrols on residential streets during all hours, MKDC planned to organize local youths to patrol on mopeds during the afternoon and early evening hours, augmenting the civilian car patrols. However, this project component had to be dropped because of changes in New York State legislation mandating vehicle inspection and registration, insurance, and the possession of a driver's license. MKDC staff members viewed the moped patrols as the only major project failure and strongly suggest that other programs considering adoption of this component examine the restrictions imposed by state and local rules of registration.

MKDC planned to establish tenant patrols in lobbies of all apartment buildings where tenants were organized and where such patrols would be both feasible and useful. It was decided that for a tenant patrol to be useful a building must have a sufficient number of tenants to be able to sustain a volunteer patrol effort. A building must also lack adequate security measures, such as a doorman service or a buzzer and intercom system. Volunteer tenant patrollers serve as lobby monitors who screen people seeking entry to the building. Since CB walkie-talkies do not work indoors, residents on the ground floor of buildings were recruited to make their telephone available to lobby monitors if they needed to call another resident to verify the identity of a visitor.

With regard to property protection MKDC introduced the standard crime prevention techniques, including home security surveys, Operation Identification, and automobile decals indicating the precinct and sector of the owner's residence and a color-coded circle indicating the age and sex of the principal driver. It was discovered that home security surveys usually were conducted only after a home had been burglarized. As part of its anti-crime project MKDC initiated surveys that would serve as a prevention function in advance of any burglary attempt.

In its project proposal, MKDC targeted residential burglary as a major problem. Fifty "install-it-yourself" burglar alarms were purchased and distributed to six civic associations, which lend the devices to vacationing members for a small fee.

The need for a personal noise-making device to alert others when trouble is feared was keenly felt by residents, particularly the elderly: 3,000 whistles donated to the project proved inadequate, particularly for the elderly. In response to these problems, MKDC purchased 1,700 freon-loaded "shriek alarms" that can be hand-activated to produce a piercing noise that can be heard for several blocks. Reaction to these alarms was described as phenomenal; they are distributed free to elderly citizens and slightly above cost to others. In addition, MKDC installed 157 locks free of charge to the elderly poor during its first year of operation.

Finally, MKDC engaged in crime prevention education. Grant funds were used to establish a community-based publication, the *Midwood Sentry,* that could explain the corporation's crime prevention and neighborhood revitalization activities, encourage volunteer participation, and inform readers of self-help security measures. MKDC also scheduled a weekly crime prevention course for community residents at the local high school with speakers from local police precincts. The effort was abandoned as the crime prevention technique became a central feature in the presentation at block and tenant association meetings.

A new spirit has emerged in Midwood since establishment of the MKDC. Thousands of residents are involved in crime prevention activities, there has been new investment in the areas's business districts, and rundown housing is being restored and rented to more permanent residents. The commitment of local residents and businesses to stay in the community is now strong. MKDC's success is due in large part to the dedication and hard work of its staff and volunteers and its systematic, yet flexible planning. It is also due to the political expertise of MKDC's leadership, their ability to work with police and other officials, and their knowledge of how their community can be tapped to take full advantage of its human resources. It is unfortunate that the project did not rigorously evaluate its effect on crime and fear of crime, since for that reason it could not meet the National Institute of Justice's stringent criteria for designation as an exemplary project.

STATEWIDE CRIME PREVENTION IN WISCONSIN

Wisconsin offers a textbook example of one state's struggle to affect crime within its borders. From 1969 to 1983, the Wisconsin Council on Criminal Justice, a department of the state government, had a consistent commitment to crime prevention, in terms of both planning and funding. With the exception of two years, the WCCJ's annual action and improvement plans designated crime prevention as a separate fundable program category, and from 1969 to 1980 more than $1.7 million was spent on crime prevention.[3]

According to the 1978 and 1980 WCCJ Criminal Justice Improvement and Action Plans, all crime prevention projects had to attempt to diminish the rate of at least one targeted Part I property crime. All jurisdictions requesting funds for crime prevention were to analyze local crime data to identify Part I crimes particularly problematic to that community. These crimes then would be targeted by the project.

All of the crime prevention projects funded by WCCJ were located within local police departments and coordinated by a crime prevention officer. Most projects included such activities as Operation Identification, security surveys, Crime Watch, and community education.

In 1980 the population served by WCCJ-funded crime prevention projects was 342,061, or 7.31 percent of Wisconsin's total population.

Typical project goals included: increased reporting of targeted crimes, reduction or stabilization of targeted crime rates, increased clearance rates, increased community involvement in crime prevention, increased recovery rates of stolen property, improved records management, statistical crime analysis, and the formal establishment of a crime prevention unit.

Information on targeted offenses was collected at all project sites and translated into machine-readable form. The information was divided into two samples — baseline and project. Baseline data covered targeted offenses occurring the year before the project was implemented, while project data reflect those occurring after implementation.

Analyses of these data were performed within three basic comparative frameworks: historical comparisons of the quantity and characteristics of offenses during the combined baseline and project periods; within-program comparisons (a comparison of burglary patterns of the Milwaukee area crime prevention projects with those not in the Milwaukee area); and a control group comparison (analysis of the quantity and characteristics of targeted offenses for all projects compared to identical variables for the remainder of Wisconsin). Within each comparative framework, the samples were analyzed along several dimensions of the targeted offenses; for example, the number of offenses, clearance and property recovery rates, the degree of force used, and method of detection.

The historical comparison of aggregated burglary patterns revealed several important findings. The number of burglaries increased 2.5 percent from the baseline of the equivalent project period. The combined clearance rate declined by about 40 percent during the project period. The proportion of burglaries in which some or all property was recovered declined by 21 percent during the aggregate project period. The proportion of attempted burglaries rose over 94 percent in the project period. The proportion of burglaries reported by citizens other than victims rose 179 percent. The proportion of burglaries from single-family homes declined by 25 percent, while the proportion from garages nearly doubled.

Similar analyses of theft samples produced three major findings. The quantity of thefts rose about 1 percent during the combined project period; the rate of clearances declined 12 percent; and, as with burglary, the proportion of thefts from homes declined 40 percent while the proportion from outdoor areas and garages rose 26 percent.

Finally, the combined project data were compared to analogous information from the remainder of Wisconsin during equivalent time periods. As noted, aggregate project data revealed a 2.5 percent increase in the number of burglaries during the same time period. Similarly, while combined project thefts rose about 1 percent from baseline to project periods, comparable data from the remainder of the state showed a 10.5 percent increase in the number of reported thefts. Thus, while the number of burglaries and thefts rose slightly for combined crime prevention projects, the rate of increase was considerably higher for the remainder of the state.

Based on these analyses, the WCCJ made several recommendations. The most important was that steps should be taken to establish a statewide Office of Crime Prevention. Such an office would provide equal access and treatment to cities, communities, and counties. It would offset a lack of local resources, facilitate public education on crime prevention, and provide technical assistance in project development. It also would conduct research and make recommendations on model legislation; and it would coordinate crime prevention activities with other state agencies.

It was also recommended that program language addressing crime prevention continue to stress concrete, practical strategies; that evaluation and data collection be continued to assure proper allocation of resources; that training of project staff should continue during and after WCCJ funding; and finally, that project resources be focused on those crime prevention strategies that show a positive impact.

PLANNING AND EVALUATION: A SUMMARY

A decade and a half of experience suggests the following ingredients for effective community crime prevention planning:

The community to be protected first must be defined. This may be a relatively simple task in a rural area, small town, or suburb, but in a large urban area administrative units or police precincts may not correspond to residents' perceptions of the boundaries of their community. Most urban programs define the community in an arbitrary manner. No matter what definition is used, however, the program will have to cultivate a sense of community among residents, who must be convinced that they are fighting a common battle.

The community's needs must be carefully assessed to make the most of limited resources. Surveys of residents and consultation with community leaders, police, and government officials may help to identify the crime problem and to target specific crimes. A more comprehensive analysis may require a survey of a random sample of neighborhood residents to assess such things as victimization, fear of crime, and attitudes toward law enforcement and criminal justice. Detailed analysis of the crime problem will not only aid in planning the crime prevention program but can also be used to motivate citizen participation.

Input must be sought from community leaders and from police and government officials. All important elements of the community must be consulted to help ensure that the program is widely accepted.

In addition to defining the crime problem, crime prevention planners need to set goals and objectives and design strategies to achieve them. There must also be provisions for evaluating the project as it is implemented and for modifying it as needed.

Most crime prevention programs establish reduction of crime in the community as their goal. A more realistic goal, however, may be a reduction in the growth of crime or in fear of crime. A precise statement of goals, objectives, and strategies is important for both planning and evaluation, and as the project progresses such a statement can help in obtaining financial support.

Local residents are the foundation of all community crime prevention programs. Collective action by citizens is what makes these programs work. Citizens must be the prime souce of information about the nature of the crime problem and they may have suggestions about how to deal with it. They can inform planners what aspects of a contemplated project may be unacceptable to the community.

Planners should devise ways of sustaining interest in the crime prevention effort to avoid burn-out of volunteers. This can be achieved through distribution of information on the success of the project, awards and special commendations to volunteers, enrollment in block and other civic associations, and continuous contact and support. Existing civic associations and community groups can help a project to stimulate and sustain community interest, so early contacts with these groups is important and an ongoing advisory group may be useful. Planners should take into account the practical concerns of such groups, the experience of their leaders, and their potential contributions to crime prevention. The new program should not duplicate, compete with, or displace existing programs.

Involvement and support of law enforcement is crucial to success. Police can provide guidance and expert advice, help legitimize the project in the eyes of the community, and provide crime statistics to help the project evaluate its impact. Planners must anticipate that police may view a community crime prevention program as amateurish and ineffective and that their reaction may be one of open hostility, particularly toward those aspects of the program that resemble patrol work or involve the monitoring of police services. A community crime prevention program may be more successful if former police officers are on staff and if representatives of the police department are assigned the task of collaborating with the neighborhood program.

There is a danger, on the other hand, that a citizen crime prevention program may become too closely identified with the police, which alienate citizens in some communities. Planning must balance police support and cooperation with citizen control. The relationship with government also is sensitive. Official support can help to legitimize a new program, but it must not be understood by residents to mean that government controls the program, particularly in communities where government-sponsored efforts are suspect.

The financial costs of community crime prevention must be considered at every stage of planning. Actual costs will be difficult to determine in advance, and financial resources inevitably will fall short of the expectations of project staff. As federal support for new community programs dwindles, planners must turn to alternative funding sources. Contacts with community, government, and business leaders can be used to locate whatever government and private funds are available.

Evaluation and monitoring should be part of any community crime prevention program. Monitoring simply means keeping track of program activities (e.g., number of crime prevention meetings, number of patrols, number of escort service runs, number of home security surveys conducted). Evaluation asks whether those activities are having the intended effects. Sources of evaluation information include: police crime statistics, surveys of neighborhood residents (particularly attitudinal surveys), surveys of police personnel, victimization surveys, observation in the neighborhood, and census data. While monitoring can be conducted by regular project staff, evaluation can be complicated and it may be useful to have specialized help from researchers attached to the local university or police department.

Planners also may consult the research reports of community crime prevention programs examined in the previous chapter in order to learn from previous efforts. Professional research outfits may be too costly to use for overall evaluation of a small program, but they may be affordable for answering specific questions.

Planners must be aware that no research design will always produce unambiguous results, and that interpretation of the data may prove complex and tricky. A number of monographs, articles, and documents are available to aid in the evaluation effort.[4]

FOOTNOTES

1. Great Britain, Home Office, *Coordinating Crime Prevention Efforts,* by F.J. Gladstone. London: Her Majesty's Stationery Office, 1980, 74 p. (Home Office Research Study No. 62).

2. The information on the Midwood Kings Highway Project was extracted from: U.S. National Institute of Justice, The *Neighborhood Fight Against Crime: The Midwood Kings Highway Development Corporation,* by William DeJong and Gail A. Goolkasian. Washington, D.C.: 1982, 98p. For additional information on the project, contact: Midwood Kings Highway Development Corporation, 1416 Avenue M, Brooklyn, N.Y. 11230.

3. Wisconsin Council on Criminal Justice, *Crime Prevention and the Wisconsin Council on Criminal Justice: 1969-1980, with Special Emphasis on Twelve Projects.* Madison: 1980, 195p.

4. In addition to the studies described in the previous chapter, the following are useful documents for evaluations of community crime prevention programs: Michael D. Maltz, *Evaluation of Crime Control Program.* Washington, D.C.: Justice Department, 1972; Donald T. Campbell and Julian C. Stanley, *Experimental and Quasi-experimental Designs for Research.* Chicago: Rand McNally, 1970; Wesely G. Skogan, "Community Crime Prevention Programs: Measurement Issues in Evaluation," in: U.S. National Institute of Law Enforcement and Criminal Justice, *How Well Does it Work? Review of Criminal Justice Evaluation 1978.* Washington, D.C.: U.S. Government Printing Office 1979, pp. 135-170; U.S. National Institute of Justice, *Partnership for Neighborhood Crime Prevention,* by Judith D. Feins. Washington, D.C.: 1983; U.S. National Institute of Justice, *supra* note 2.

CHAPTER 9

THE DISPLACEMENT PHENOMENON

In earlier chapters it was suggested that crime displacement may account for the success of some crime prevention programs. Although crime may be reduced in one area at a specific time, there may be displacement to other areas, other targets, or other times. As we have seen, some experiments report definite displacement, others report no displacement, and still others find no evidence one way or another. One thing is certain: the phenomenon is difficult to measure.

A national evaluation of the effects of 60 street-lighting projects found the measurement of displacement to be complicated by the fact that many lighting projects are installed in conjunction with other law enforcement programs such as improved neighborhood patrols. This evaluation concluded that there is no proof that street lighting affects the level of crime, but there is evidence that uniform lighting decreases the fear of crime.[1] A study of street lighting in Kansas City, however, found that installation of improved lighting in a single block appeared to move crime, such as robbery, to adjacent areas.[2] Similarly, a study of the effects of added manpower in one New York City police precinct on crime rates found that the increase may have reduced street robbery in the target area while incresing it in neighboring precincts.[3]

And an eight-year study in New York City found that after an increase in police patrol in the subways, a sudden increase in the number of robberies of bus drivers diminished the number of subway robberies below the levels that would otherwise be expected. Requiring exact change on buses virtually eliminated robberies of bus drivers, and subway robberies returned to anticipated levels. Robbery apparently was displaced first away from and then toward the subways because of the changes in the relative attractiveness of buses and subways as targets for robbers.[4]

Displacement in time was the subject of a study of the effect of a 10 p.m. to 6 a.m. curfew imposed on juveniles in Detroit in the summer of 1976. While crime in August during the curfew hours was lower than normal for that time, it was above normal in the afternoon, particularly from 2 p.m. to 4 p.m. The curfew reduced crime while it was in effect, but there was a distinct displacement to other hours of the day.[5]

The smaller the geographical area in which crime control programs are established the greater should be the problem of displacement. A network flow model for measuring displacement was illustrated with sample arrest data spanning an entire year obtained from the Crime Analysis Team in Atlanta. Application of the model revealed a significant displacement of criminals from the suburbs to the inner city but not from the inner city to the suburbs.[6]

The displacement hypothesis also was tested in an evaluation of an Operation Identification program. Would the program shift criminal activity from the homes of participants to those of non-participants? Would criminals turn from residences to businesses? And would they show a preference for unmarked rather than marked property? There was statistically significant evidence of the first of these three forms of displacement, and some minor support for the other two.[7]

The most useful analysis of displacement is presented by Repetto, who classifies displacement into several broad types: temporal, tactical, target, territorial, and functional. He rejects the hypothesis that reducing opportunities and increasing the risks of crime are of no value because they merely displace crime, suggesting that there are distinct limits to criminal displacement. Suppression of crime in one area should not produce a complete displacement to other areas, but should result in a major reduction in the target area and only a modest increase elsewhere. Also, some crimes are purely opportunistic and preventing them in one circumstance will not lead to their displacement to another, and offenders may not operate as effectively in another area or be as proficient in another type of crime.[8]

In sum, the research suggests that criminal displacement can be a problem, but that an anti-crime strategy's displacement potential can be gauged in advance and, in certain circumstances, minimized.

FOOTNOTES

1. U.S. National Institute of Law Enforcement and Criminal Justice, *National Evaluation Program Phase I Report: Street Lighting Projects.* Washington, D.C.: U.S. Government Printing Office, 1979, 102p.

2. Roger Wright and others, *The Impact of Street Lighting on Street Crime.* Ann Arbor, Mich.: 1974.

3. New York City Rand Institute, *Some Effects of an Increase in Police Manpower in the 20th Precinct of New York City.* New York: 1971, 158p.

4. New York City Rand Institute, *The Impact of Police Activity on Crime: Robberies on the New York City Subway System.* New York: 1974, 74p.

5. Lee A. Hunt and Ken Weiner, "The Impact of a Juvenile Curfew: Suppression and Displacement in Patterns of Juvenile Offenses," *Journal of Police Science and Administration,* 5(4): 407-412, 1977.

6. Stuart J. Deutsch and others, "A Network Flow Model for Forecasting and Evaluating Criminal Displacement," *Evaluation Quarterly,* 3(2): 219-235, 1979.

7. Thomas Gabor, "The Crime Displacement Hypothesis: An Empirical Examination," *Crime and Delinquency,* 27(3): 390-404, 1981.

8. Thomas A. Repetto, "Crime Prevention and the Displacement Phenomenon," *Crime and Delinquency,* 22(2): 166-177, 1976.

CHAPTER 10

CRIME PREVENTION THROUGH ENVIRONMENTAL DESIGN

The concept of "defensible space," pioneered by Oscar Newman in the 1970s, suggests that residential neighborhoods can reduce crime by creating the physical expression of a social fabric that defends itself.[1] The physical environment can be designed to support the social control of crime through such mechanisms as real and symbolic barriers, strongly defined areas of influence, and improved opportunities for surveillance. In effective combinations, these mechanisms can bring an environment under the control of its residents.

Newman examined housing developments in every major city in the United States, concluding that the urban environment itself has been the criminal's best ally. He points out mistakes in architectural housing development design that victimize residents and specifies the means by which such mistakes can be avoided. His layout of the multi-family dwelling, from the arrangement of the building grounds to the interior grouping of apartments, was designed to allow residents to perceive and control all activity taking place within it. Newman's defensible space design, while using mechanical prevention, intended to formulate an architectural model of corrective prevention.

In a second book, entitled *Design Guidelines for Creating Defensible Space,* Oscar Newman prepared a set of guidelines for architects, developers, housing agencies, and community groups to aid in addressing the problems of security in residential environments at the design and planning stage.[2] He analyzes four types of buildings for their suitability for residents of different ages, family structures, backgrounds, and lifestyles. He shows how residents of different ages and lifestyles use their environments, and how these different uses open up their homes to crime and vandalism. The design guidelines are intended to make different types of buildings secure for different types of residents.

89

Newman's concept of Crime Prevention Through Environmental Design (CPTED) assumes that a combination of security hardware, psychology, and site design can prevent crime. CPTED aims to reduce opportunities for crime through attention to territoriality, surveillance, lighting, landscaping, and physical security. The physical environment includes the structure of buildings and the layout of neighborhoods and streets.

Many of the defensible space designs recommended by Newman were in subsequent years built into housing projects or high-rise buildings. However, such buildings have been gradually replaced by townhouses with shared open space instead of private front and backyards. Newman shows that the greatest opportunities for crime are found in shared open space, arguing that good surveillance and a clear definition of territoriality boundaries can make such space more defensible.

A study of 75 surburban townhouse developments in northern California found many departures from the defensible space ideal. Among the recommendations for improvement was that developments should be subdivided into smaller clusters of houses, clearly labeled and sharing a well-defined area of open space and parking.[3]

DEFENSIBLE SPACE AND CRIME

Several studies have tested Newman's concept of defensible space for its impact on crime. One study analyzed the effect on crime of environmental factors in two matched samples of urban households. In one sample the residents had been victims of vandalism or burglary during the 18-month period before the study. In the second sample the residents had not experienced any offense. The households were matched on type of dwelling, minority status of residents, household composition, years in school, and age. Analysis of the data produced mixed results. Defensible space was effective in deterring crime in indoor public areas, but not in outdoor areas, and it was found to have only a slight effect on residents' feelings of responsibility for public areas.[4]

An environmental survey based on Newman's territoriality and surveillance standards was applied to six townhouse developments with 2,219 units in Sacramento, California, and survey scores were compared to the crime rate. Unexpectedly, the townhouses with the "best" defensible design scores had higher crime rates than did townhouses with "good" defensible space. One possible interpretation of the finding is that residents who have the best defensible space environments feel more secure and are thus more vulnerable.[5]

Another study examined the conditions under which residents of a housing project act or fail to act to defend both defensible and non-defensible space. The research consisted of 18 months of participant observation of a small inner-city housing project in an Eastern port. The researcher regularly socialized with ten families and interviewed one member of two-thirds of the households about thier experiences with victimization, their expectations that someone would help them, and their own intervention in crimes. A questionnaire was administered to 101 individuals selected to represent the categories of ethnicity, age, sex, and length of residence in the project: 40 Chinese, 23 blacks, 18 whites, 13 hispanics, and seven others. The questionnaire examined attitudes toward crime and danger as well as knowledge of the identities of local teenagers and experiences with victimization.

The study focused on the low-rise portion of the project where 300 brick garden apartments cluster around quiet dead-end courtyards. The development is a microcosm of urban diversity. Ten years of co-residence have failed to forge its diverse population into a cohesive community. Networks of friends and kinsmen fall within ethnic boundaries, and social cleavages between ethnic groups are sharp.

Superficially, the housing development was well designed for defensible space, yet crime is extensive and most residents have adopted security precautions. Architectural strategies thus are not enough to prevent crime. Spaces may be defensible but not defended if the social apparatus for effective defense is lacking. Even if buildings are low, with entrances and public spaces clearly linked to particular apartments (as recommended by Newman's guidelines), residents will not respond to crimes if they feel that the space belongs to another ethnic group, if they believe that the police will come too late or they will incur retribution for calling them, or if they are unable to distinguish potential criminals from a neighbor's dinner guest. Residents often fail to intervene in crime because of the fragmented social organization of the housing project, its pervasive anonymity and fear, the prevalance of stranger relationships among by-standers and a sense of futility about calling the police.

A minority do intervene, however. They are residents with extensive urban experience and familiarity with street life, with widespread social networks within the project, a commitment to the neighborhood, a sense of belonging to a socially dominant group, and a sense of mastery over the hazards of their environment.

The study suggests that enthusiasm for crime control through environmental design should be tempered. Defensible space design may lead to disappointing results when the social fabric necessary for defensive behavior and the institutional supports for effective intervention, such as an adequate police force, are absent. Defensible space is a necessary but not sufficient condition for crime prevention. The study concludes that the relationship between environmental and social behavior is complex and reciprocal since the environment itself is defined by the ways its users interpret it and impose on it their own cultural meanings.[6]

The most extensive experiment of CPTED was conducted in Portland, Oregon, in a program designed to reduce crime and fear of crime in an urban commercial strip and adjacent, residential areas. The program included not only physical modifications but support from police, local merchant groups, and social organizations. The project site was a three and one-half mile commercial strip, the Union Avenue Corridor (UAC), in northeast Portland. The street was characterized by vacant lots, boarded-over windows, derelict structures, and night spots of dubious reputation. The UAC also had a disproportionate share of the city's crime problems, and local businessmen felt that crime was the single greatest obstacle to the successful operation of their businesses.

A number of tactics were implemented to bring about changes in the physical and social environments, including commerical and residential security surveys, redesign of streets and intersections, installation of high-intensity street lighting, building of new bus shelters, organization and support of the Northeast Business Boosters, Sunday Market and Clean-up Days, assistance to other environmental changes, and public transportation for the handicapped and the elderly.

Changes in the crime rate were monitored through police reports and victimization surveys. Changes in fear of crime were measured by self-report items on questionnaires and interviews and by observation of the use people made of the area's facilities. Data on changes in quality of life were drawn from city business files and from interviews with businessmen concerning their perceptions of the economic vitality of the area.

CPTED in Portland was judged to be a moderate success in the business environment and a lesser success in the residential environment. The increase in physical security was high for business areas but low for residential areas. Other measures, such as increased crime prevention activity or community cohesiveness also showed greater success for commercial than for residential areas. Reported crime data showed that commercial burglary and robbery were reduced after the commercial security surveys, so CPTED was thus at least partially responsible for a reduction in UAC's crime rate. And CPTED certainly contributed to resident's optimistic outlook about the UAC.[7]

The Portland CPTED project was judged sufficiently important to rate a second study in 1981 to determine which aspects of the program had lasting effects after the project had formally ended. CPTED was judged to have been moderately successful in changing the physical and social environments. The program was most successful in increasing access control and surveillance. Target-hardening efforts and improved street lighting were maintained through the post-project period, and businesses were organized into a cohesive group that worked toward preventing crime and revitalizing the commercial strip. There were, however, no indications of a similar degree of social cohesion in the residential community.

CPTED's ultimate goals were to reduce crime and fear of crime and to improve the quality of life. For these long-range goals, the second evaluation found some improvements that could be attributed to the CPTED program. The most important findings was a significant decrease in commercial burglaries, attributed to the security survey and street-lighting programs. The decreases were sustained for the two-year follow-up period. No decreases in street crimes, commercial robbery, or residential burglary could be attributed to CPTED activity. Fear of crime within UAC appears not to have changed substantially since the end of the CPTED demonstration. Residents and businessmen were still somewhat fearful, especially during night hours. The most successful strategies were judged to be the security advisor services and the organization of the community around crime prevention programs. The least successful were, ironically, the massive architectural changes planned for Union Avenue. The lessons learned from the experiment were that CPTED goals must be realistic, that an implementation period of five years most likely will be necessary, and that a strong organizer and facilitator must oversee the work.[8]

The concept of CPTED was applied in yet another demonstration project which attempted to reduce school crime in Broward County, Florida. Crime problems in the county's school system were assessed, and efforts were made to enhance student identification with the school and to increase the risk of committing crimes. School yards, bicycle parking area, hallways, stairways, restrooms, locker rooms, and school grounds were renovated to increase opportunities for surveillance. Access to isolated areas was limited, transitional and functional areas were clearly defined, and natural borders were introduced in accordance with Newman's concepts. An evaluation using student attitude questionnaires and school crime records showed moderate increases in movement control, surveillance, activity support, and student motivation reinforcement. No significant change in student perceptions of safety was found, although there was a modest reduction in crime victimization.[9]

Finally, a review of the link between crime and the built environment examined 52 studies of the last decade. Findings support the conclusion that elements and combinations of elements of the physical environment can reduce both crime and fear of crime. Most effective were means of control such as locks, alarms, and surveillance cameras. Factors that increase visibility also were important. There is no explanation for the effects on crime or fear of crime that do occur. The review concludes that it is not yet possible to predict whether a crime prevention strategy will be effective and thus to suggest which strategies to use. However, many of the design features suggested by the CPTED theory are inexpensive (such as better locks) and some (such as fewer families per building) are desirable in themselves.[10]

CONCLUSION

The moderately successful CPTED program implemented in Portland resembles those described in the chapter on community crime prevention, and the architectural improvements were judged the least successful component of those programs. Organization of the community around crime prevention was judged the most important.

Defensible space apparently has only a weak relationship to crime. Judicious architecture, in itself, does not seem to be the key to a crime-free environment. Rather, the physical design of defensible space must compete with a number of other factors, among which are the commitment of residents to controlling their own environment and the quality of outside management. Defensible space programs are successful only as part of a larger and more comprehensive crime prevention program that includes police support and residential anti-crime activities.

FOOTNOTES

1. Oscar Newman, *Defensible Space: Crime Prevention through Urban Design.* New York: MacMillan, 1972, 234p.

2. Oscar Newman, *Design Guidelines for Creating Defensible Space.* Washington, D.C.: National Institute of Law Enforcement and Criminal Justice, 1975, 213p.

3. Dennis J. Dingemans and Robert H. Schinzel, "Defensible Space Design of Housing for Crime Prevention," *Police Chief,* 44(11): 34-36, 1977.

4. Alan Booth, "The Built Environment as a Crime Deterrent: a Reexamination of Defensible Space," *Criminology,* 18(4): 557-570, 1981.

5. Dennis J. Dingemans, "Evaluating Housing Environments for Crime Prevention," *Crime Prevention Review,* 5(4): 7-14, 1978.

6. Sally E. Merry, "Defensible Space Undefended: Social Factors in Crime Control through Environmental Design," *Urban Affairs Quarterly,* 16(4): 397-422, 1981.

7. U.S. National Institute of Justice, *Crime Prevention through Environmental Design: the Commercial Demonstration in Portland, Oregon.* Washington, D.C.: U.S. Government Printing Office, 1980, 60p.

8. U.S. National Institute of Justice, *A Re-evaluation of Crime Prevention through Environmental Design in Portland, Oregon.* Portland, Oregon: Office of Justice Planning and Evaluation, 1981, 48p.

9. U.S. National Institute of Justice, *Crime Prevention through Environmental Design: the School Demonstration in Broward County, Florida.* Washsington, D.C.: U.S. Government Printing Office, 1980, 74p.

10. U.S. National Institute of Justice, *The Link between Crime and the Built Environment—the Current State of Knowledge (Vol. 1),* by C. Murray and others. Washington, D.C.: U.S. Government Printing Office, 1980, 110p.

CHAPTER 11

CRIME PREVENTION
THROUGH GUN CONTROL

Gun control is one of the most controversial issues in the United States today. Opponents and advocates of gun control both cite research on the effects of gun control legislation to support their positions. Unfortunately, evidence can be assembled to support almost any position regarding the issue. The truth is far more elusive than the studies imply.

Readers who wish to become more familiar with the pros and cons of the issue and with the intricacies of the methodological research questions involved in gun control should consult the May 1981 issue of the *Annals of the American Academy of Political and Social Science.*[1] Here we will look at the most recent studies of the effects of gun control on violent crime.

GUN CONTROL AND CRIME

In 1976 a document issued by the U.S. Comptroller General pointed out that 63.8 percent of murders, 23.6 percent of aggravated assaults, and 42.2 percent of robberies in the United States were committed with guns. In that year, the FBI reported that guns were used in approximately 320,000 of these crimes. The Comptroller General noted that over the previous ten years the use of guns in crime had increased greatly and that there was evidence of a direct relationship between handgun availability and gun-related crimes. Stringent gun control laws, the report concluded, may not reduce the number of violent attacks, but the severity of attacks would be reduced since less lethal weapons would be used. If guns were less readily available, there would be a decrease in murder and an increase in crimes classified as aggravated assault.[2]

A comprehensive state-of-the-art review of firearms and violence was issued recently by the Social and Demographic Research Institute of the University of Massachusetts. The report notes that the stock of private firearms in the United States increased from 80 million in 1968 to about 120 million in 1978. Contrary to common belief, there was no evidence that fear of crime and violence was an important factor in the increase. Roughly three-quarters of the private firearms stock is owned primarily for sport and recreation; the remainder, for protection and self-defense. Gun owners tend to be male, rural, southern, Protestant, affluent, and middle class.

The Institute found no evidence of a strong causal relationship between private gun ownership and the crime rate. Crime may be a motivating factor in the purchase of some protective weapons, but these constitute no more than one-quarter of the total private stock. There was no compelling evidence that private acquisition of weapons is an important cause of, or a deterrent to, violent crime. It is commonly hypothesized that such criminal violence, especially murder, occurs because the means of lethal violence is readily at hand. The Institute, contradicting the Comptroller General's report, found no presuasive evidence to support this conclusion.[3]

SOME STUDIES OF GUN CONTROL LEGISLATION

One of the most extensively researched gun control laws in the United States was the Bartley-Fox law, which went into effect in Massachusetts in April 1975. This law preserved the general structure of the state's gun control statutes, but added a mandatory maximum one-year sentence for those convicted of illegally carrying a firearm. The law also prohibited suspended sentences, probation, and various informal means of avoiding the mandatory sentence.[4]

The effect of the law was assessed through an analysis of reported crime data from the FBI's *Uniform Crime Reports* and the Boston Police Department. An interrupted time series research design allowed comparison of Massachusetts crime trends with those for the United States as a whole and for North Central, Middle Atlantic, and the New England regions individually; crime trends in Boston with those of other comparably sized cities of the New England, Middle Atlantic, and North Central regions; and crime trends in Massachusetts cities and towns excluding Boston with those in comparable cities and towns for each of the regions. The impact of the law was studied for 1975, 1976, and 1975-76 combined.

Introduction of the Bartley-Fox law had an immediate, two-fold effect on armed assault in Massachusetts. First, it substantially reduced the incidence of gun assaults even before its effective date and second, it substantially increased non-gun assaults. The findings thus supported the Comptroller General's contention that stringent gun control would reduce the severity of attacks since less lethal weapons would be used. From 1974 through 1976, the Massachusetts gun assault rate declined by 19.6 percent, which can be compared with declines of less that 5 percent for all the other jurisdictions studied (except for the Middle Atlantic states, which showed a 12.6 percent decline). In Massachusetts, non-gun armed assaults increased by 24.1 percent from 1974 through 1975, while gun assaults decreased by 15.7 percent. In Boston, gun assaults with battery fell by 37.1 percent in the two years following implementation of the law. From 1974 through 1976 gun assaults were about 23 percent of armed assaults in Massachusetts. After the gun law went into effect they dropped to 16 percent of the total, a 30 percent reduction.

The law produced an estimated reduction of 355 gun assaults in Boston and 427 gun assaults in Massachusetts excluding Boston, or a total reduction throughout the state of 782 gun assaults, in 1976. However, gun control accounted for increases in non-gun assaults of 907 in Boston and 539 outside Boston in Massachusetts, or 1,446 throughout the state by 1976. The displacement effects of the law were more than twice its deterrent effects in Boston, while deterrent effects were about the same as displacement effects for the state outside Boston.

The gun law had a moderate deterrent effect on gun robbery in 1975 in Boston and an even lesser effect outside Boston in Massachusetts. In 1976, however, the deterrent effect of the law was much more pronounced and was approximately equal within and out-side Boston. The proportion of robberies involving guns decreased by 22 percent in 1974-76, a larger decrease than in any of the comparison areas that were studied. By 1977, on the other hand, there was in Boston the beginning of a shift back to using guns in robberies in certain types of targets such as street, taxi, and residential robberies.

It was estimated that the law resulted in a reduction of 300 gun rob-beries in 1975 and 569 in 1976, or an estimated reduction of 870 gun robberies in Boston by 1976. There also was an increase of approx-imately 594 non-gun robberies in 1975 and 253 in 1976 for a total in-crease of 846 non-gun robberies in Boston by 1976. For Massachusetts excluding Boston, it is estimated that the law deterred 539 gun robberies and resulted in an increase of 227 non-gun robberies during 1975-76.

Analysis of the law's effect on homicide was restricted to Boston and its control jurisdictions. The law did seem to have a deterrent effect on gun homicides, but there was no indication of displacement to non-gun homicides. During 1974-76 Boston experienced a 56 percent decline in gun homicides, a much larger decline than any of eight comparison jurisdictions.

The study concluded that the Bartley-Fox law has affected the character of crime in Massachusetts. There have been substantial decreases in gun-related assault, robbery, and homicide, and at least partially offsetting increases in non-gun armed assault and robbery. This represents a shift from more serious to less serious forms of criminal activity, since crimes are more likely to result in injury and death when committed with guns.

It could not be determined how the law accomplished these effects — whether by the threat of punishment or by its imposition. It is not known whether the observed effects were the result of the certainty and severity of punishment under the new law, the altered way in which the criminal justice system is handling such cases, or the impression the new law has made on the public apart from any changes in criminal justice processing.

Arrests for illegal gun-carrying did decrease after passage of the law. There were 218 such arrests in 1974, 186 in 1975, and 168 in 1976. There was no evidence of any widespread evasion of the law by Boston police officers, who might have been hesitant to arrest someone carrying a gun because of the minimum one-year jail sentence. There was some confusion over the difference between "carrying" and "possessing" a firearm (the former was subject to the mandatory minimum sentence while the latter was not), and charging policy varied from one jurisdiction to another.

The proportion of defendants who were convicted of illegally carrying a firearm decreased after Bartley-Fox, but the proportion of these who received some jail sentence increased. However, it was estimated that for one full year in Boston no more than about 40 individuals went to jail who would not have been jailed before passage of the law.[5]

The firearms control act of 1975 of the District of Columbia was the subject of a study by the United States Conference of Mayors. The comprehensive law banned the sale of handguns to civilians, froze the number of firearms in the District, and required a thorough background investigation of persons registering weapons. It is one of the strictest gun control laws in the United States.

A comparison of the rate of firearm-related homicide, robbery, and aggravated assault in the District of Columbia for the three years before the act with the three years after its implementation showed that all three categories decreased significantly. Handgun homicides decreased 26.2 percent, assaults with handguns 10.5 percent, and robberies with handguns 22.5 percent. In addition, deaths by firearm accidents dropped from a rate of 0.3 per 100,000 in 1974 and 1975 to virtually zero in 1978 and 1979. The suicide rate decreased 40 percent. Comparisons with the United States as a whole, the South, and all cities with populations between 500,000 and one million also showed that the District of Columbia had the greatest decrease in crime rates in all three categories.[6]

The Conference of Mayors report was subjected to re-analysis by another researcher who pointed out deficiencies in the research method as well as the use of unrealistic assumptions. This analyst concludes that, at most, the act may have been responsible for a reduction in handgun fatalities related to arguments. The percentage of handgun homicides related to felonies actually increased, suggesting that the act is no panacea for crime.[7]

In 1979 Canada's Ministry of the Solicitor General commissioned a study of the effectiveness of Canada's new gun control provisions. The legislation is designed to reduce the number of incidents involving firearms through provisions concerning the screening of applicants, prohibition of gun ownership, regulation of businesses dealing with firearms and ammunition, search and seizure, and sentencing.

The study found that the use of firearms declined since introduction of the new law, but this simply continued a trend started in the mid-1970s. Crimes involving the use of knives as an alternative to guns did not increase. The clearest positive results of the new law were found in firearms suicide rates, which declined significantly in the first full year of the new law's implementation in metropolitan Toronto.[8]

The broadest social experiment undertaken by any Western society to curb gun crimes was the 1974 Gun Court Act of Jamaica. During the 1960s the reported incidences of shooting-with-intent and of murder were about 6 to 7 per 100,000 population. In 1974 the reported incidence of shootings-with-intent had increased by 1,900 percent and that of murders 400 percent, with gun murders accounting for at least 50 percent of the total. Under the Gun Court Act, persons found guilty of gun charges would be placed in indefinite detention in a special prison until a review board recommended release. Analysis of the incidence of gun crimes for a one-year period before and after passage of the law showed a decline of 56 percent from 124 to 55. The greatest decline, 78 percent, occurred over the first six months following passage of the legislation; the 22 percent decline in the second six months was not statistically significant. There was an increase in other types of murder from 99 to 144. The overall murder rate declined by 14 percent from 1973-74 (n = 232) to 1974-75 (n = 199).

There was a 37 percent decline in shootings-with-intent, from 879 to 556. The drop was again greatest over the first six months, but was significant for both six-month periods. There was a 28 percent decline in the number of armed robberies from 1,893 to 1,369, a statistically significant decrease. The decline increased during the year following the Gun Court Act. Robberies without the use of a gun declined 58 percent in the first six months and increased by 30 percent in second six months.

The researchers concluded that the decrease in gun crimes was not an artifact of an overall decrease in crimes reported to police. Some crimes continued to increase slightly while others dropped or fluctuated.[9]

Apparently contradicting the Massachusetts and Jamaican experience is a study of the relationship between gun control and homicide rates. Data from two previous studies were used to determine whether or not strict gun control laws have a deterrent effect on homicide. Data on the homicide rates in 47 of the 52 largest cities in the United States for 1963-65 and 1971-72 were applied to a Guttman scale of strictness devised for gun control laws in the United States for 1968. Elements of the laws analyzed included minimum age requirements, license to carry a concealed handgun, license to sell handguns, sales reported to police, waiting period between purchase and delivery, license to purchase a handgun, and license to own a handgun.

This study showed that states with stricter gun control statutes tended to have higher homicide rates and a greater increase in the homicide rate during the time period studied. This association was found both for the overall strictness of the statutes and for several of their individual elements. It was unclear whether a high and rising homicide rate motivates state legislatures to pass strict control statutes, or whether gun control statutes have no preventive effect on homicide.[10]

CONCLUSION

In general, research has found the effects of gun legislation to be moderate or nonexistent, or to dissipate over time, although there are exceptions. Researchers often disagree over the meaning of their findings or the assumptions on which they are based.

It may well be that very strict gun control laws (such as those of England and Japan where private ownership of handguns has been virtually eliminated) are directly responsible for the exceptionally low homicide and violence rates in those countries. Such severe restrictions, however, may not be acceptable to the American public. Although majorities of the American population have favored licensing or registration of firearms, especially handguns, they have not supported a total ban on private ownership. There are already 20,000 gun laws on the books in the 50 states, yet more than 120 million firearms remain in private hands.

Many writers have warned of the unacceptable social costs of enforcing unpopular gun control laws, including a substantial amount of lawbreaking. It may take a decline in the social status of the handgun in the home to create an atmosphere favorable to a sharp reduction in the growing inventory.

FOOTNOTES

1. "Gun Control," *Annals of the American Academy of Political and Social Science,* 455:1-167, 1981.

2. U.S. Controller General, *Handgun Control: Effectiveness and Costs.* Washington, D.C.: 1978, 90p.

3. U.S. National Institute of Justice, *Weapons, Crime, and Violence in America,* by James Wright and Peter H. Rossi. Washington, D.C.: U.S. Government Printing Office, 1981, 41p.

4. Glenn L. Pierce and William J. Bowers, *The Impact of the Bartley-Fox Gun Law on Crime in Massachusetts.* Boston: Center for Applied Social Research, 1979, 151p.

5. David Rossman and others, *The Impact of Massachusetts' Mandatory Minimum Sentence Gun Law.* Boston, Mass.: Boston University School of Law, Center for Criminal Justice, 1979, 17p.

6. United States Conference of Mayors, *The Analysis of the Firearms Control Act of 1975: Handgun Control in the District of Columbia.* Washington, D.C.: 1980, 33p.

7. Edward D. Jones, *The District of Columbia's Firearms Control Regulations Act of 1975: The Toughest Handgun Control Law in the United States—Or Is It?* Washington, D.C.: U.S. Justice Department, 1981, 18p.

8. Canada, Solicitor General, *Evaluation of the Canadian Gun Control Legislation. First Progress Report.* Ottawa, Ontario: 1981, 166p., app.

9. Paul Gendreau and C. Thomas Surridge, "Controlling Gun Crimes: the Jamaican Experience," *International Journal of Criminology and Penology,* 6(1): 43-60, 1978.

10. David Lester and Mary E. Murrell, "The Relationship Between Gun Control Statutes and Homicide Rates: a Research Note," *Journal of Crime & Justice,* 4:145-147, 1981.

CHAPTER 12

MASS MEDIA CRIME PREVENTION CAMPAIGNS

Several countries, among them the United States, Canada, Britain, and the Netherlands, have recently initiated national campaigns to encourage the public to take precautions against particular kinds of crime and to enlist citizen action in preventing crime generally.

In the United States the National Citizen Crime Prevention Campaign is a nationwide public education and technical assistance program with four major objectives: to change unwarranted feelings about crime and the criminal justice system, particularly feelings of frustration and hopelessness; to generate among citizens a sense of responsibility for crime prevention; to encourage citizens, working within their community and with local law enforcement, to take collective action; and to aid in developing crime prevention programs at local, state, and national levels. The campaign, sponsored by 44 national nonprofit organizations, 14 federal agencies and 30 state agencies, provides a support network for communities, businesses, and citizens groups seeking to combat crime. The media portion of the campaign, under the auspices of the Advertising Council, features a trench-coated, animated dog named McGruff.

Two independent studies were conducted to assess the effect of the media effort on the nationwide audience. The first was conducted soon after its initiation (1980), the second two years later. The first study sought to answer three questions: Can mass media communications motivate the general public to participate in crime prevention activities? If so, what empirical bases are there on which to forge control strategies for effective public communications on behalf of crime prevention? And what specific control strategies (including themes, appeals, and message targets) evolve from an evaluation of pertinent theories, principles, and data?

Phase 1 of the study focused on the McGruff public service advertising campaign to "Take a Bite Out of Crime". Preliminary findings from panel and national samples suggested that the campaign reached sizeable proportions of citizens in its early stage, and had various effects on at least some of them. Exposure to the McGruff advertisement was more likely among people who perceived themselves as vulnerable to crime, particularly members of the lower socioeconomic groups, who are ordinarily less concerned about crime prevention. Nationally, those exposed were likely to be young males and generally more attentive to public service advertisements.

The campaign was judged most effective in generating concern about crime prevention, and in helping to convince those exposed to do more about it. Exposure to the campaign did not have discernible effects on citizens' sense of personal responsibility for preventing crime, their confidence that they could protect themselves, what they thought they knew about prevention, or how effective they thought their prevention activities might be. Those exposed to the Advertising Council campaign were more likely to see themselves as having a need for such information. Attitude and behavior changes were more likely among people who said they needed information and who paid attention to it when they received it. Thus, exposure to the McGruff campaign seems to have had some meaning for those who feel they benefit from public education campaigns in general.

No single strategy, the report concludes, is likely by itself to persuade a heterogeneous group of people to take crime prevention actions across the board. However, a public information campaign directed to the public at large can be effective in persuading certain subgroups (mostly affluent citizens) to take one-time actions to protect their property. Person-protection actions requiring self-confidence and repeated use are likely to encounter more difficulty.[1]

The second evaluation of the "Take a Bite Out of Crime" campaign was based on a sample of 1,188 adults interviewed during November 1981, nearly two years after the campaign was launched. This study examined the extent of citizens' exposure to the campaign and their reactions to it, particularly their own perceptions of its effects on their behavior.

Fifty-two percent of the national sample of respondents could recall having seen or heard at least one of the public service announcements, as compared to 30 percent a year and a half earlier. One-third of these reported having seen the ads more than ten times. The announcements appear to have reached sizeable numbers within all demographic subgroups, but age was the dominant predictor of exposure to the campaign: Over two-thirds of those under 35 recalled the ads, while only one-third of those over 65 did. The campaign appeared to be diffusing throughout the population, rather than simply reaching the same audience repeatedly. Even among the least media-attentive segments of the population, campaign exposure was substantial. Over 25 percent of respondents said they had paid a great deal of attention to the ads, while 75 percent said they paid at least some attention. A strong majority perceived the ads as effectively conveying their message. More than half said that they had made them more concerned about crime and more confident in protecting themselves. Twenty-two percent said the ads made them more fearful of being victimized, with women more likely to report this than men. Again, public information efforts appeared to reach people who are more concerned about crime and who report a need for information about prevention.[2]

Somewhat different findings were obtained from a study of a media campaign in Alberta, Canada. Residents of that province were surveyed before the campaign began and after it had been in operation for one year. Large numbers of Albertans were found to have been exposed to the campaign, but a considerably smaller number perceived its themes and messages as salient and only a few altered their behavior as a result. Thus, while the program may have overcome the physical barriers to communication, it did not overcome the more important psychological barriers. Analysis of monthly crime statistics for one city found that variations over the campaign period could be explained in terms of seasonal patterns rather than campaign influence. In other words, the media campaign did not reduce crime.[3]

In the Netherlands nationwide media campaigns focusing on crime prevention were conducted in 1977 and 1978 to encourage citizens to take precautions against particular kinds of crime. In 1979 a victimization survey was used to gauge the effect of the campaign on public awareness and behavior. Some 68 percent of survey respondents were able to recall one or more of the public service announcements. Crime prevention efforts were taken by 12 percent of the total population as a result of the campaigns. The campaigns particularly affected urban residents, residents of higher socioeconomic status, and residents under age 55. The latter two findings corresponded to the experience of the American McGruff campaign. The advertisements were found particularly effective in preventing car theft, bicycle theft, and breaking and entering offenses.[4]

MEDIA CAMPAIGNS AND CRIME

While the above studies provide useful insights into the effect of mass media campaigns on the public, they do not reveal their effects on crime (except, to some extent, the Alberta study). This was the focus of two studies by Britain's Home Office, one of an anti-vandalism campaign in northwest England in 1978, the other of a car-security campaign in northern England in 1979.

The anti-vandalism campaign was aimed at both deterring youngsters from vandalism by emphasizing the risk of being caught, and in instilling in parents the need to supervise their children. Television advertisements, each lasting about 45 seconds, were aired during one three-week period and one five-week period. One advertisement was aimed at boys between 9 and 13 years of age and the other at the parents of young boys.

The study found no evidence of a significant effect on parents' attitudes toward vandalism or on the amount of vandalism committed. There were comparable decreases in vandalism against schools and phone booths in both test and control regions, while house vandalism did not seem to have been affected. These results matched those of other offender-oriented advertising campaigns, and two reasons were given for the failure: Offenders are unlikely to be moved by generalized threats unless they have reason to believe that the actual risks and consequences of detection are worsened; in addition, remote advertising messages cannot compete with immediate pressures operating as an offense is committed.

The car-security campaign took the form of two separate advertising projects, both directed mainly at the owners of older cars without steering-column locks. The first used television advertisements in northeast England, the second used press and poster advertisement in northwest England. Both campaigns ran for eight weeks.

None of the measures used to evaluate the campaign showed any benefits unequivocally attributable to the advertising. Although the number of auto crimes decreased somewhat in the press and poster campaign area, the decrease was less than in the control area. Analysis of stolen vehicle reports showed a significant decrease in thefts of newer vehicles in the press and poster campaign area when compared to the control area, but in the television campaign area there was no apparent reduction in thefts of either older or newer cars. Security checks on parked cars did not suggest that car owners in either of the campaign areas had become more conscientious about locking their cars.[5]

CONCLUSION

In general, mass media campaigns for crime prevention have reached large numbers of people, generating concern about crime prevention and increasing the disposition of those exposed to do something about it. While a few people say they have changed their behavior as a result of a campaign, spot checks have not shown this to be so. Two studies of the effects of media campaigns on crime found no evidence of crime reduction.

The greatest potential of the mass media in crime prevention may lie in directing citizens toward better information and motivating them to get involved in collective action. Lavrakas believes that the McGruff campaign described above is a step in the right direction since the public needs to relearn their responsibilities for preventing crime. The real value of the campaign, in his view, is that it serves an important legitimizing function for the efforts of local agents as they take the crime prevention message to their communities.[6]

FOOTNOTES

1. University of Denver, Center for Mass Communications Research and Policy, *Public Communications and the Prevention of Crime,* by Garret J. O'Keefe and Harold Medelsohn. Denver: 1981, 2 vols.

2. University of Denver, Center for Mass Communications Research and Policy, *Citizen Reactions to the "Take a Bite Out of Crime" Campaign After Two Years: a National Survey Evaluation.* Denver: 1982, 40p., app.

3. Vincent F. Sacco and Robert A. Silverman, "Selling Crime Prevention: the Evaluation of a Mass Media Campaign," *Canadian Journal of Criminology,* 23(2): 191-202, 1981.

4. Netherlands, Justice Ministry, *Crime Prevention: an Evaluation of the National Publicity Campaigns,* by Jan J.M. van Dijk and Carl H.D. Steinmetz. The Hague: 1981, 32p.

5. Great Britian, Home Office, *Crime Prevention Publicity: an Assessment,* by D. Riley and P. Mayhew. London: Her Majesty's Stationery Office, 1980, 47p. (Home Office Research Study No. 63).

6. Paul J. Lavrakas, *Citizen Self-Help and Neighborhood Crime Prevention.* Evanston, Ill.: Northwestern University, Center for Urban Affairs and Policy Research, 1982, 44p.

CHAPTER 13

CRIME PREVENTION
IN OTHER COUNTRIES

MARXIST (SOCIALIST) METHODS OF PREVENTING CRIME

Marxist ideology proclaims that the everyday problems of crime cannot be dealt with until capitalism is abolished and replaced by a socialist society free of class struggle. According to Marxist criminology, crime and criminal justice are an integral part of the historical development of capitalism and will become unnecessary under socialism. But how well has Marxist theory held up in practice? By locating its existence in an ideal future, Marxism renders itself immune from empirical criticism. Its main assumptions, untestable in the real world, are designed to suspend the relationship among history, theory, and social reality.[1]

Marxist criminology can be analyzed, however, as a theory of what is and as an ideology of what ought to be. Any ideology can be tested against other ideologies and real societies. Such a comparison would reveal that societies based on Marxist ideology are unjust and oppressive, though contemporary Marxist criminologists ignore that fact. Without exception, countries that have embarked on the kind of society advocated by them are totalitarian in nature, use repression far more readily than democratic societies, and have a ruling class that is far more oppressive than do most capitalist societies.

Let us look at some crime prevention measures taken by countries based on Marxist principles. In the United Nations journal, *International Review of Criminal Policy,* Ivan Timoshenko, a Soviet official, describes measures taken against crime in the USSR with case material from the Byelorussion SSR. His article begins with a recital of basic Marxist tenets vis-a-vis crime: Under socialism, he claims, there is an opportunity to eliminate crime and its causes altogether. The preconditions for success are created by the course of historical development and depend on the improvement of social relations, an increase in the political activity of the masses, and their involvement in the production process.

Part of the program of the Community Party of the Soviet Union is the elimination (not simply reduction) of crime. Instances of crime that still exist, according to Timoshenko, can be explained by an individual's "moral perversion", intellectual backwardness, low level of culture, or degradation of alcohol. In the Marxist scheme of things crime in capitalist societies has its roots in social causes, while in socialist societies the source of crime is found in the individual.

Timoshenko recites official statistics for White Russia: Crime there has declined 27.4 percent from 1940 to 1970. Thefts are reported to have declined fourfold and the incidence of "hooliganism" twofold. Timoshenko claims a 500 percent reduction in the number of persons sentenced for crimes. The types of crimes still remaining to be "eliminated" are illegal production of alcohol and misappropriation of public property. Any growth of individual crimes is the result of improved detection work by the militia and public agencies. Timoshenko claims that today there is no gangsterism, no organized crime, no robberies, no kidnappings, no hijacking of aircraft, no sale and use of narcotics, and no racial discrimination.[2]

Intended for the Western reader, a book entitled *The Problems of Crime in the USSR* looks at the topic through the eyes of one of its natives schooled in criminology. The picture that emerges is different indeed from that presented by official propaganda. Using data and research from various sources the Soviet criminologist calculates the incidence of crime in the USSR for the period 1972-74 at 16 to 20 million crimes per year, or two times more than in the United States. Based on data for 1972, he calculates the overall number of criminal court convictions at about 1.6 million. The exact number of prison inmates in the USSR is not known, but Soviet officials have admitted to 800,000 inmates in 1960 or four times the number of inmates then in American prisons. In the early 1970s, based on a study of satellite photographs, the United States Central Intelligence Agency determined that the camp and prison population was about 2.5 million. In 1978 Shifrin reported that in that year there were about 3,000 prisons, correctional labor camps, and colonies that held about 5 million prisoners.[3]

The reality of crime in Soviet society shows no evidence of the steep decline claimed by Timoshenko and official propaganda. Despite the emphasis by Soviet authorities on preventing crime, no dramatic decrease in any kind of crime has been observed. The government centrally coordinates a national and local crime prevention effort with an elaborate penal system. According to Soviet ideology it is the moral duty of all citizens to aid in the eradication of crime, a necessary prerequisite to the establishment of full communism. Yet, despite the official emphasis on participation of the "collective" in preventing crime, a permanent job and residence are the strongest deterrents for both first offenders and recidivists.[4]

There is a distinct geographic distribution of criminality in the USSR which differentiates Soviet crime from that of both developing and industrialized countries. In the USSR increasing urbanization is not correlated with higher rates of crime. The internal passport system and the difficulties of moving to large cities have affected Soviet crime in two ways. First, they have shifted criminality away from the large older cities to the newly established cities of the far east and the far north and to the rapidly expanding smaller urban centers. Second, the communities surrounding major cities are not the privileged suburbs of the prosperous that they are in the United States but the homes of young men (the most crime-prone sex and age category) forced to commute long hours under unfavorable conditions to their schools and jobs. Population controls and the internal passport system, the essential Soviet tools for controlling crime, have resulted in a distribution of crime which is fundamentally different from that found in most industrialized countries. A reduction of crime in the major Soviet cities has been achieved at the cost of reduced personal freedom and increased problems of crime in more remote parts of the country.[5]

Often cited as causes of Soviet juvenile delinquency are bad family influences, delinquent peer groups, unemployment, contact at work with older workers who steal from their employers, decadent books and films, and bourgeois (Western) propaganda. Delinquency prevention efforts rely on a supportive and sanctioning network of social agencies, block and apartment house committees of neighborhood activists who work with "morally unstable" people, Komsomol (Communist Youth League) organizations, volunteer People's Guard detachments, lay judges, factory committees, and trade union committees. Any of these individuals or agencies can refer delinquents or misbehaving parents to nonprofessional Comrades' Courts within housing offices or at work places.[6]

Compared with American criminal justice, the Soviet system is tightly woven and centrally coordinated. In recent years, the goals of the criminal justice system of the USSR have shifted from repression by terrorism to crime prevention through education and to an emphasis on individual duty in law enforcement. The militia (police), created in 1917, has been mandated to prevent crime through intelligence activities, direct intervention, and citizen education. In 1966 it was given the responsibility for direct supervision of offenders newly released from correctional institutions. Volunteer brigades aid the militia in crime prevention, and inmates as well as citizens have "a national duty to mind other people's business."[7]

Apart from the survival of most traditional crimes, the new revolutionary order in the Soviet Union has given rise to new types of crime. Drug and traffic offenses are increasing today, while organized crime, despite Timoshenko, survives in small groups of a professional criminal underworld. It has grown among corrupt officials engaging in economic crime, official crime, and "crimes against socialist property." Workplace crime reaches down from the highest party posts and ministerial levels to factories, farms, construction outfits, shops, storerooms, and counters. Pilfering state property is the most widespread of all offenses.[8]

An interesting case study is presented by crime and crime prevention in Communist East Germany. Since World War II both adult and juvenile offense rates have been substantially lower in East than in West Germany. While crime has been rising in the West, official East German statistics show a steady decline: 500,000 crimes were reported in 1946, 230,000 in 1950, and 109,000 in 1970. In 1970 the official crime rate in East Germany was 640 per 100,000 population, in West Germany 3,924.

East German Communist criminologists see the trend as proof of the superiority of the socialist system over the "decadence" of the capitalist system. Apart from questionable statistics, an analysis of differences in urbanization and industrialization in the two states suggests how demographics have contributed to the divergent crime rates. The population of East Germany declined from 18.3 million in 1950 to 16.9 million in 1973; West Germany's increased from 50.2 to 61.9 million in the same period. East Germany's population density decreased from 170 people per square kilometer to 157; West Germany's increased from 205 to 249. Significantly, the 1973 population of juveniles in East Germany was 88.7 percent of what it was in 1950. West Germany is more highly urbanized and industrialized than East Germany. A very large part of East Germany's productive population, and thus of the most crime-prone age group, has fled to the West since World War II.

In the mid-1970s East Germany reached the limits in its attempt to "eradicate" crime and delinquency, and the influences of social class, educational status, place of residence, and sex on the crime rate remain intact even in this totalitarian state, one of the world's most oppressive. Under Marxist ideology such influences should be overcome in a socialist system, yet since 1968 the reported crime rate has registered increases and the government has responded by increasing penalties.[9]

Yet another example of crime prevention within a Marxist system is presented by a study of Communist Cuba, 20 years after Fidel Castro's revolution. The study finds that crime control agents are present throughout Cuba, including police and the Committees for the Defense of the Revolution. Despite this pervasive control, traditional forms of crime are flourishing. As in the Soviet Union, there are new types of crime, including black market crimes, labor crimes such as "loafing", absenteeism, "underproduction", and misappropriation and embezzlement of state property.

Property crimes, particularly thefts involving money and marketable goods, constitute the greatest proportion of overall crime committed in Cuba, and have risen in recent years. Robbery is the second most frequently reported crime, accounting for 13 percent of all arrests in 1977. Organized rings are involved in both stealing and disposing of property. Juvenile delinquency is concentrated among lower-class male youths with low educational achievement who come from broken homes. Other features of juvenile delinquency in Cuba are the existence of gangs, which are very similar to those found in capitalist countries, and adults working in collusion with juvenile delinquents.

The prevalence in Cuba of a "machista" culture, weakening of family life, instability produced by the new economic and political order, and increasing rates of serious crime indicate that the system's socialization and crime prevention efforts have largely failed. In many ways, the Cuban experience resembles that of other societies, both Marxist and capitalist. Marxism has not helped Cuba reduce its crime problem.[10]

THE JAPANESE EXPERIENCE

Post-war Japan is the world's greatest success story in crime prevention, in spite of its rapid industrialization and urbanization.

From 1962 to 1972 there was a 20 percent reduction in total crime. If simple theft is excluded, then in these ten hectic years of extensive urban migration and industrial development, there was an incredible decline in the serious crime rate of no less than 40 percent.

Searching for an explanation of this phenomenon, one of Australia's foremost criminologists points to the racial homogeneity of the Japanese population and traits peculiar to Japanese culture. People trust the police and the judiciary; family and neighborhood control of behavior are strong; tradition stresses the obligations and duties of the individual rather than his rights; people accept their duty to assist or supplement the authorities in crime prevention and the reclamation of criminals; the work ethic reduces labor conflicts; and a belief in personalized rather than abstract justice permits a tolerance of less serious forms of deviance.

Since World War II the Japanese have achieved a balance between freedom and justice that permits the country to grow, industrialize, and urbanize without the worst disruptions of crime. The first lesson to draw from the Japanese experience is that it is not based on religion, ideology, or nationalism, and that it is imposed from above rather than a "grass roots" development. The current demand in Western countries for community alternatives to the official system of crime control is a belated realization of the need for simpler solutions to crime. Japan offers a way of keeping social organization simple within the context of a huge and complex metropolis. The Japanese, in effect, have the kind of community within which successful informal control can be exercised.

The Japanese method may not suit those in Western countries who seek the privacy and anonymity of urban living and prefer to be unconstrained, but it provides the Japanese the kinds of protection urban dwellers in other countries are now seeking.[11]

A DUTCH CRIME PREVENTION EXPERIMENT

A crime prevention project in The Hague, reminiscent of some of the more successful police-community crime prevention programs in the United States, confirms American findings that citizen-police cooperation reduces victimization, at least among those who participate.

A burglary control team of two detectives and eight constables of the municipal police force in one district consisted of foot and bicycle patrols, provision of information on burglary prevention, and response to reports of burglaries. Forty percent of residents in the district knew of the burglary team's existence, but 60 percent did not, despite extensive newspaper publicity. Residents who knew of the burglary team reported burglaries far more often than those who did not. As in the United States, the experiment stimulated willingness to report crime — not only burglary but all crimes against property.

Residents who were aware of the team claimed more often to have taken steps to prevent burglary, and those given information and advice on crime prevention by members of the team were more willing to report crime.

Victim surveys showed that incidents of burglary remained the same or dropped slightly in the experimental district. Elsewhere in The Hague and the rest of the Netherlands sharp rises were reported. The role displacement may have played is not reported.

The research concluded that the most likely reason for the success of the experiment was the team's concentration on burglaries and the publicity, which deterred potential burglars.[15]

CONCLUSION

Official claims of substantial crime reductions in Communist countries are highly suspect. What objective studies are available in the West do not support the view of sharp, systematic reductions in the crime rate. Studies conclude that crime in the USSR is rampant, and the large number of prisoners in correctional institutions and camps hardly indicate that it is abating. Traditional crimes in Communist countries continue to flourish and some new forms of crime, such as "theft of socialist property" have been added to the list. A lower crime rate in East Germany compared to its Western counterpart is in large part due to the large numbers of young adults who fled to the West after World War II, as well as to other demographic and economic factors. Crime prevention in Cuba has been a failure.

Japan's startling success in controlling crime can be attributed to its racially homogeneous population, the Japanese tradition of trusting and obeying authority, and the sense of community and duty to the group. Crime prevention experiments in the Netherlands and Britain are largely in conformity with findings of similar programs in the United States.

FOOTNOTES

1. Carl B. Clockars, "The Contemporary Crises of Marxist Criminology," *Criminology,* 16(4): 477-515, 1979.

2. Ivan O. Timoshenko, "Collaboration of the Militia and the Community in Crime Prevention in the Byelorussion Soviet Socialist Republic," *International Review of Criminal Policy,* 33:39-44, 1977.

3. Ilya Zeldes, *The Problems of Crime in the USSR.* Springfield, Ill.: Charles C. Thomas, 1981, 140p.

4. Louise Shelly, "Soviet Crime Prevention: Theory and Results," *Prison Journal,* 58(2): 60-67, 1978.

5. Louise Shelly, "The Geography of Soviet Criminality," *American Sociological Review,* 45(1):111-122, 1980.

6. Peter Juviler and Brian F. Forschner, "Juvenile Delinquency in the Soviet Union," *Prison Journal,* 58(2):18-30, 1978.

7. David W. Patterson and Ann Duak, "Criminal Justice in Soviet Russia," *International Journal of Comparative and Applied Criminal Justice,* 4(2):113-124, 1980.

8. Peter H. Juviler, *Revolutionary Law and Order: Politics and Social Change in the USSR.* New York: Free Press, 1976, 274p.

9. Arnold Fieiburg, "Zur Iugendkriminalitaet in der DDR" (Juvenile Delinquency in the German Democratic Republic), *Kolner Zeitschrift fur Soziologie und Sozialpsychologie,* 27(3):489-537, 1975.

10. Louis Salas, *Social Control and Deviance in Cuba.* New York: Praeger, 1979, 398p.

11. William Clifford, *Crime Control in Japan.* Lexington, Mass.: Lexington Books, 1976, 200p.

PART IV.

PREVENTION OF INDIVIDUAL CRIMES

Part II of this volume examined comprehensive juvenile deliquency prevention programs; Part III looked at comprehensive crime prevention programs with emphasis on police and community crime prevention. This section will provide information on the prevention of specific crimes or crimes against specific target populations (such as the elderly) with an emphasis on identifying resources available to the reader.

CHAPTER 14

ARSON

In 1981 more than 11,000 law enforcement agencies representing 86 percent of the U.S. population reported 122,610 arson offenses to the FBI. Agencies reported arson clearance data showed a 15 percent clearance rate.[1]

A year-long congressional investigation of arson-for-profit in the United States concluded that arson is virtually out of control. During 1978 insurance companies paid out $1.6 billion for losses caused by arson. Along with the obvious effects of arson, insurance companies increase their premiums to help absorb their losses, and city welfare agencies must relocate burned-out families at public expense. Organized crime now uses arson as a regular source of income. Hired "torches" have increasingly turned to burning down businesses and homes because law enforcement agencies have traditionally been weak in arson detection. The arson business draws its profits from insurance payoffs. Insurers often provide coverage on properties for much more than their real value, thus making arson-for-profit highly lucrative. Insurance companies are increasingly challenging suspicious claims, however, reducing the freedom with which arson profiteers generally operated in the past.

The absence of a unified effort by local, state, and federal law enforcement and criminal justice agencies has helped the epidemic of arson in the United States. Because arson detection and control traditionally has been a local law enforcement problem, federal agencies have not coordinated their efforts to prevent this kind of crime. In addition, prosecutors are not anxious to devote time to arson cases, primarily because of the difficulty in proving their allegations.[2]

PREVENTING ARSON

A National Institute of Law Enforcement and Criminal Justice study of arson prevention included a survey of all fire departments in cities with a population of 50,000 and on-site observation of six departments. New York was found to have made extensive use of arson patrols in the South Bronx and developed a program to coordinate the arson investigation process under the Bronx district attorney. Philadelphia has developed a cooperative relationship among police, fire, prosecution, and the federal Arson Task Force. Seattle has combined a strong public relations campaign with arson patrols and a cooperative investigation effort. Denver and Dallas have mounted aggressive public relations efforts, and New Haven has focused on the development of an arson early warning data system with the cooperation of the insurance industry.

Efforts to prevent arson have been constrained by the low priority traditionally given this crime by the community, law enforcement departments, and fire control agencies. This is exacerbated by the complexity of the crime, which actually includes any number of distinct and unrelated fire-setting behaviors, each of which may demand very different resources from government, the community, and public protection agencies. Finally, arson control programs have been hampered by a lack of knowledge about the true incidence of the crime. The recommended strategies of the NILECJ report stress a well-coordinated investigation and prosecution process.[3]

Since December 1979, 11 federal agencies have been cooperating to detect and investigate arson rings, provide training for arson investigators, support community actions against arson, revise regulations and procedures of insurance companies, and educate the public about arson prevention and control. By 1981 there were 117 arson task forces nationwide and 26 arson strike force teams in selected cities. Nine major arson-for-profit rings were exposed by federal arson strike teams, and seven cities developed arson information management systems to predict arson-caused fires.[4]

A 1982 *Arson Resource Directory* identifies key organizations and individuals who are active in arson prevention and control.[5] And anti-arson implementation kits, based on knowledge gained from successful programs, are available to aid local planners in designing programs for arson control.[6]

FOOTNOTES

1. U.S. Federal Bureau of Investigation, *Uniform Crime Reports for the United States, 1981.* Washington, D.C.: U.S. Government Printing Office, 1982, pp. 33-35.

2. U.S. Senate, Governmental Affairs Committee, Permanent Subcommittee on Investigations, *Arson in America.* Washington, D.C.: U.S. Government Printing Office, 1979, 73p.

3. U.S. National Institute of Law Enforcement and Criminal Justice, *Arson Prevention and Control: Program Model,* Washington, D.C.: U.S. Government Printing Office, 1980, 132p.

4. U.S. Fire Administration, *A Report to the President on Progress in Implementation of the National Arson Strategy.* Washington, D.C.: U.S. Government Printing Office, 1981, 132p.

5. U.S. Fire Administration, *Arson Resource Directory.* Washington, D.C.: 1982, 308p.

6. U.S. Federal Emergency Management Agency, *Arson Task Force Assistance Program: Anti-Arson Implementation Program.* Washington, D.C.: U.S. Government Printing Office, 1980.

CHAPTER 15

AUTO THEFT

In 1981, the second year of a slight decline in this offense, vehicle thefts were occurring at a rate of 469 per 100,000 population. Nationally, an average of one of every 150 registered cars was stolen in that year. The average value of stolen vehicles was $3,173, for an estimated total loss of $3.4 billion. Today only 40 percent of all vehicles stolen are ever recovered, compared to 10 percent a decade ago. A decade ago also, the teenage joyride was a major source of auto theft; today, adults organized in auto theft rings steal on order and for "chop shop" parts.

The National Association of Investment Insurers reports that from 1970 to 1980 car thefts in the United States dropped from 830 to 690 per 100,000 vehicles. Despite this decrease, insurance costs for auto thefts have increased. The NAII has proposed that the problem be dealt with locally rather than through standard remedies applied nationwide. The insurance industry should institute, the NAII recommends, make, model and territorial ratings of auto theft coverage. Insurers should offer competitive discounts for anti-theft devices of proven effectiveness; they should lobby for better state laws and seek export controls and revisions of racketerring statutes at the federal level; and they should use pre-insurance vehicle inspection and special investigative units with discretion.[2]

Auto theft investigators have supported the Motor Vehicles Theft Prevention Act, which mandates that vehicle identification numbers be stamped on every major component of a vehicle, not just the engine and transmission. Some states, including New York and Massachusetts, have been cracking down on legal loopholes that allow professional auto thieves to thrive.[3]

Andrew Karmen suggests that the victim's negligence as a cause of automobile theft has been exaggerated. The proportion of at-risk cars that are vulnerable because keys were left in the ignition ranges from 0.5

percent to 6 percent of all automobiles stolen. Karmen argues that the preoccupation with thefts aided by careless owners is a form of scapegoating by officials in the automobile and insurance industries and in law enforcement. In his view, officials blame the victim for making their cars easier to steal in order to divert attention from those who design and insure cars that are easily stolen.[4]

The California Highway Patrol reports a successful Auto Theft Reduction Program that has reversed the upward trend in auto thefts and aided in the recovery of stolen vehicles. The program's success is attributed to improved Highway Patrol investigative techniques, selective inspection of suspect vehicles, closer surveillance of auto dismantlers and junk yards, and improved patrol officer training and education. The program involves coordination of California's entire law enforcement network.[5]

FOOTNOTES

1. U.S. Federal Bureau of Investigation, *Uniform Crime Reports for the United States, 1981.* Washington, D.C.: U.S. Government Printing Office, 1982, p. 39.

2. National Association of Independent Insurers, *Reducing Auto Theft: a Five-point Plan.* Des Plaines, Ill.: 1982, 36p.

3. Bernard Edelman, "Auto Theft: For Police, the Joy Ride is Over," *Police Magazine,* 3(5): 16-21, 1980.

4. Andrew Karmen, "Victim Facilitation: the Case of Automobile Theft," *Victimology,* 4(4): 361-370, 1980.

5. Glen Craig, "The California Highway Patrol Auto Theft Reduction Program," *Journal of California Law Enforcement,* 10(1): 13-16, 1975.

CHAPTER 16

BURGLARY

In 1981 over 3.7 million burglaries were reported to law enforcement agencies in the United States for a rate of 1,632 per 100,000 population. Burglaries accounted for 28 percent of the FBI's index crimes and 31 percent of all property crime. Residential property was targeted in 67 percent of reported burglaries; non-residential property accounted for the remaining 33 percent. The national burglary clearance rate was 14 percent. Victims of burglary suffered losses estimated at $3.5 billion, and the average dollar loss per burglary was $924.[1]

The real impact of burglary, of course, transcends these figures. The frequent occurrence of this crime contributes to the perception of general lawlessness that has altered the way Americans live. Yet effective prevention is in many cases as simple as locking up before leaving home. The National Crime Survey reports that many burglaries are committed impulsively by non-professionals who enter through unlocked doors or windows.[2]

Burglary is the crime most frequently targeted by the kind of comprehensive prevention efforts described in Chapters 6 and 7. This chapter will describe burglary prevention programs that are not part of a more comprehensive effort. These include police concentration on the activities of narcotic addicts (who typically rely on burglaries to support their habits) and on narcotics trafficking, anti-fencing operations, projects to recover stolen property, security surveys, and public school burglary reduction programs.

A study of the Narcotics Addict Control Project of the Santa Barbara Police Department (which enforces provisions of criminal and health and safety codes against the use of narcotic drugs) tested the notion that jailing active narcotic addicts would reduce thefts and burglaries. Robberies, forgeries, and other crimes committed by addicts to maintain their addiction also were expected to decrease. Three separate evaluations were conducted to measure the effect of this project. The first compared the incidence of burglary and larceny in Santa Barbara County for two years before the project and for the 12-month experimental period with experience in a control group of cities with similar social, demographic, and environmental characteristics. The second test compared property crime in Santa Barbara County, exclusive of offenses committed in the city, with the crime rate that would have prevailed if incarceration rates of addicts had remained unchanged. The third test was a comparison of county-wide property crime levels, including those in the city of Santa Barbara, with the levels that would have prevailed if the number of addicts incarcerated had been only those normally apprehended by the Sheriff's Narcotic Task Force.

The experiment was judged to be successful. Offense levels in Santa Barbara County did go down, for both larceny and burglary. The average monthly reductions were between zero and 3.7 percent for laceny and between 11.2 and 24.7 percent for burglary, and a decline in related offenses probably took place as well.[3]

The El Monte (California) Police Department undertook a similar six-month experiment to interrupt narcotics trafficking. During the experimental period the burglary rate was 32.3 percent lower than in the previous six-month period, and 24 percent lower than in the six-month period following the program. The degree of burglary suppression seemed to vary with the emphasis of the different shifts on narcotics offenses, and there was some displacement to nearby communities. A regional burglary program was later established to prevent displacement.[4]

An example of a successful burglary prevention program by means of security surveys is presented by Oregon's Multnomah County commercial burglary prevention project. Between July 1977 and June 1978 the county conducted nearly 500 commercial security surveys. Each participating business was contacted by a deputy who completed a thorough internal and external security assessment. A few days after the survey, a report of the premise inspection, including recommendations for improvements, was mailed to each participant.

Six months after the survey each business was telephoned to determine whether the recommendations had been implemented. To measure the effect of the survey on the level of burglaries, 435 program participants and 225 businesses that were not surveyed were examined for reported burglaries one year before and one year after the survey program.

A time-series analysis of monthly burglary totals for both the target group and the control group showed a significant reduction in burglary following compliance with the target-hardening recommendations. There were 97.6 percent fewer burglaries in businesses with a compliance rate of at least 76 percent, as compared to the nonparticipating control group. Unfortunately, the significance of this finding was diluted due to the small-size of the high-compliance group ($n = 27$) and the high variability in the number of burglaries per business in both high-compliance and control groups. However, another analysis showed that Multnomah County had experienced a slight decline in burglaries since inception of the program, while a nearby county without such a program showed a significant increase during the same period.[5]

A pilot program designed to reduce unlawful garage entries and home burglaries was tested in St. Louis. It was assumed that if homeowners who leave their garage doors open were informed by police that such behavior was strongly associated with garage burglary, then these crimes could be prevented. Patrol officers made lists of homes at which open garage doors were spotted, and letters were sent to the resident. Using information on garage burglaries before and during the experiment and for a similar neighborhood without such a program, the department was able to show that garage burglaries decreased by 32 percent. However, the control group experienced an identical decline, illustrating the difficulties that are often associated with the measurement of program effectiveness.[6]

The Burglary Coordinator Program in Siskiyou County, California, is a county-wide information retrieval system using Instant Data System cards in a modus operandi file of all burglary cases. Its purpose is indirect burglary prevention through increased rates of recovery of stolen property and increased clearance rates. Each card in the file is coded and retrieved according to such factors as type of burglary, characteristics of the offender, year of the offense, or disposition of the case.

In its first year of operation the clearance rate for burglaries increased by 77 percent over the preceding 12 months; the arrest rate increased by 38 percent. In the first year also 31 percent of property reported stolen was recovered, and 54 percent recovered the second year. Burglary in the second year decreased by 6 percent, and there were increases in arrests for burglary of 30.5 percent for adults and 10 percent for juveniles.[7]

Yet another effort to affect the incidence of burglaries in the United States is a federal anti-fencing program. Initiated in 1974 by the Law Enforcement Assistance Administration, this program assists law enforcement agencies in developing a capability to conduct undercover operations. The objectives of the program are to apprehend thieves, fences, and other criminals associated with the handling and disposal of stolen property. Transactions are videotaped, providing prosecutors with the best evidence possible and resulting in a high rate of quilty pleas and significantly reduced court costs.

In the first three years of the program 62 operations have been conducted in 39 cities. They have resulted in 7,228 indictments against 4,600 individuals ranging from street thieves and fences to major organized crime figures, white-collar criminals, and corrupt officials. More than $130.6 million worth of stolen property has been recovered with an outlay of only $4.1 million in "buy money." Over 90 percent of defendants have pled guilty.[8]

The Illinois Legislative Investigating Commission believes that the best way to curb fencing and burglary is to amend the Criminal Code to authorize civil action for fencing of stolen merchandise for three times the amount of actual damages. The commission also proposes legislation allowing punitive damages, creating certain statutory presumptions, and precluding the raising of issues and defenses.[9]

FOOTNOTES

1. U.S. Federal Bureau of Investigation, *Uniform Crime Reports for the United States.* Washington, D.C.: U.S. Government Printing Office, 1982, pp. 21-24.

2. U.S. National Criminal Justice Information and Statistics Service, *The Cost of Negligence: Losses from Preventable Household Burglaries.* Washington, D.C.: U.S. Government Printing Office, 1979, 32p.

3. Harold L. Votey, "Narcotic Addict Control in Santa Barbara County: an Evaluation of Effects on Property Crimes," *Journal of Police Science and Administration,* 9(2): 150-159, 1981.

4. Phillip L. Moore and others, *First Priority: Narcotics Traffic; Reducing Residential Burglaries by Targeting Heroin-Related Offenses.* Claremont, Calif: Claremont McKenna College, 1982, 14p.

5. Oregon Law Enforcement Council, *Portland Public Schools Burglary Prevention Project: Final Evaluation Report.* Salem: 1977, 65p.

6. Ron Pennington, *An Evaluation of the Open Garage Door Burglary Program.* St. Louis, Mo.: St. Louis County Police Department, 24p.

7. Phillip Summers, "The Burglary Coordinator Program is Working in Rural Community," *Crime Prevention Review,* 6(4): 18-22, 1979.

8. U.S. Law Enforcement Assistance Administration, *Taking the Offensive: Property Crime Law Enforcement through Undercover Anti-Fencing Operations: A Special Report.* Washington, D.C.: 1978, 26p.

9. Illinois Legislative Investigating Commission, *Fencing: Criminal Redistribution of Stolen Property.* Chicago: 1978, 70p.

CHAPTER 17

CRIMES AGAINST CHILDREN

Physical or psychological abuse and neglect, sexual molestation, incest and related offenses comprise this category of crimes against children. The number of reported cases of child abuse and neglect continues to rise, with the actual number of cases being much higher than reported. According to the latest federal survey, over 1.1 million children are abused or neglected each year, and 2,000 children die from resulting injuries or conditions. Although public awareness of child abuse and neglect has increased and improvements in dealing with it have been made, much more needs to be done, with prevention rather than treatment as the emphasis.[1]

A study in New York City suggested that many cases of child abuse and neglect could be prevented if the staffs of government and private agencies were trained to identify and deal with parents with child-rearing problems. At-risk parents — those who may abuse or neglect a child — display early warning signals, sometimes even before the child is born. But professionals often fail to identify these signals for a number of reasons, including limited knowledge of parenting problems, the single-purpose mission of most agencies, and work overload which leaves little time for dealing with unexpressed client needs.

The New York study revealed that at-risk parents are not isolated from helping institutions. Rather, they are frequent clients at agencies such as prenatal clinics, schools, community centers, welfare departments, employment offices, courts, hospital clinics, and drug programs.

These parents often demonstrate a sense of incompetence and poor self-esteem, difficulty in seeking and finding pleasure in the adult world, social isolation, a strong belief in the value of punishment, a family history of abuse, and a serious lack of ability to empathize with the conditions and needs of children. Such characteristics manifest themselves in visible danger signals — problem drinking, repeated job loss, unwanted pregnancies at a young age, poor medical care, birth complications, unrealistic expectations of their children, and an inability to maintain children on various behavior and school schedules — that can be spotted by trained professionals as possible precursors to physical or emotional abuse.

The lack of early identification and intervention affects both the maltreating parent and the child. Alcoholism counselors, for example, treat the parent's drinking problem, but fail to deal with the underlying child-care problems. Meanwhile, child welfare workers are separating abused children from their homes but not motivating alcoholic parents into treatment so that the needed solution can be achieved.

The solution to the child maltreatment problem lies in the early identification and treatment of the at-risk parent. Despite prevailing opinion, an early warning system already exists. With proper training and resources doctors, teachers, and social workers can help deal with the problem of child maltreatment. The Children's Aid Society of New York recommends that a training program be instituted to instruct staff of helping agencies how to identify and intervene with the at-risk parent. The Society also suggests that a national system be developed which, without impinging on anyone's civil rights, would provide a central registry of clients in need of help in order to allow agencies to identify and track at-risk parents. Both government and private agencies should aid this network by identifying families with child-coping problems.[2]

A comprehensive child abuse prevention program in Pomona County, California, is the joint effort of the Pomona Police Department and the Attorney General's Crime Prevention Unit. The project consists of three phases. Phase 1 provides in-service training in child abuse recognition, investigation, and the relationship among child abuse, domestic violence, and alcohol and drug abuse for all law enforcement, non-sworn communications, and records personnel in the county. Phase 2 provides in-house training and community awareness sessions on child abuse and associated problems, the state reporting law, and the roles and responsibilities of law enforcement. Phase 3 developed a Pomona resource directory, which identifies community services for the detection and prevention of child abuse. The Pomona project has increased the overall reporting of suspected child abuse by 30 percent and has enhanced cooperation among county agencies and resource systems in dealing with crimes against children.[3]

Another approach to the prevention of child abuse is through Parents Anonymous, a self-help group for parents who have abused or who fear they might abuse their children. Parents meet weekly with a group leader, work together to discover how to prevent child abuse, and support one another in times of crisis. Parents Anonymous also provides a crisis telephone hotline for its members. A manual presents case material on abusive parents who have joined the program and examines the ways parents can be helped to overcome their abusive behavior.[4]

FOOTNOTES

1. U.S. Comptroller General, *Increased Federal Efforts Needed to Better Identify, Treat, and Prevent Child Abuse and Neglect.* Washington, D.C.: U.S. Government Printing Office, 1980, 113p.; U.S. National Center on Child Abuse and Neglect, *Study Findings: National Study of the Incidence and Severity of Child Abuse and Neglect.* Washington, D.C.: U.S. Government Printing Office, 1981, 56p.

2. Philip Coltoff and Allen Luks, *Preventing Child Maltreatment: Begin with the Parent.* New York: Children's Aid Society, 1978, 53p.

3. Rusty Gagnon, "The Pomona Project: a Total Community Approach to Child Abuse Prevention," *Crime Prevention Review,* 6(4): 39-51, 1979.

4. Christine C. Herbruck, *Breaking the Cycle of Child Abuse.* Minneapolis, Minn.: Winston Press, 1979, 205p.

CHAPTER 18

DOMESTIC VIOLENCE

A nationwide study of 2,143 adults representing a cross-section of families in 103 counties in the United States found that violence in the family was increasing. Six thousand husbands or wives out of every 100,000 used the more serious forms of violence (punching, kicking, biting, hitting with an object, beating, or using or threatening to use a knife or gun) on one another during the years. Of the adults interviewed, 28 percent reported that the husband was the attacker. Generalizing the data to all American couples, about 1.8 million wives may be severely attacked by their husbands at least once a year. Violence is much more likely to occur in households with younger spouses, and it is affected by age, income, employment, religion, residence in a city, region of the country, and race.

The least violent homes are those with fewer than two children, where the husband and wife experience little life stress in the course of the year, and where decision-making power is shared. The highest risk of family violence occurs when there is more than one child at home, where there is considerable life stress experienced by one or both of the marital partners, and where decision-making is the responsibility of one person.[1] The major approach to preventing domestic violence and spouse abuse has been to help women to escape dangerous situations through emergency housing, legal aid, and job training leading to economic independence. A New York City study found that the most compelling reason why battered wives did not try to escape was financial dependence. Law enforcement was the type of service most often used by women in the study. Seventy percent of the women had sought medical services at least once. The study found that medical personnel, like police, could use further training on domestic violence. Actions taken in criminal and family courts resulted in some reduction of violence. One of the main responses to the problems of battered women recommended by the New York study was to expand their employment opportunities.[2]

In addition to services for victims of spouse abuse, strategies are needed for stopping the abuse at its source. Working with the battered is a difficult task, particularly because of his lack of motivation to change. The criminal justice system can provide the leverage needed to force the batterer to recognize the seriousness of his actions and to motivate him to change through threat of punishment. Developing a range of alternatives to imprisonment then becomes the responsibility of the social system.

Because a batterer may have other problems related to the abuse, such as alcoholism or unemployment, a network of services is needed to deal comprehensively with the batterer and other members of the family. Because many different types of agencies may be involved in the service network, coordination is a key function.

Although the state of the art in working with batterers is not advanced, some intervention methods and formats do show promise. New approaches to the problem, such as educational and community organization strategies, are beginning to be tested. Alternatives to incarceration for men who batter require strong links between the justice system and the social services. Monitoring the batterer's progress and feeding information back to the justice authority requires formal communication mechanisms. Lines of communication must be clear to avoid losing the client between the two systems.[3]

A community approach to domestic violence is illustrated by Detroit's Family Trouble Clinic, which provides emergency counseling to families and individuals. While the program concentrates on spouse abuse, it also provides services in cases of child abuse, elder abuse, parent abuse by a minor, violence between siblings, runaway adolescents, and suicidal threats. The program is a cooperative effort between the Family Service of Detroit and Wayne County and the Detroit Police Department.

Service is available seven days a week through a regular full-time staff during the day and an on-call part-time staff at night and on weekends. This program thus provides services not available before, a factor that is considered one of its strongest features. Police and social work skills are combined, yet the two disciplines maintain those qualities that make them different professions. The service has demonstrated its usefulness with both affluent and lower socioeconomic groups; it has made effective use of telephone casework service; and it has demonstrated skillful use of outreach to help a new and difficult client population.[4]

FOOTNOTES

1. Murray A. Strauss and others, *Behind Closed Doors: Violence in the American Family.* Garden City, New York: Anchor Press/Doubleday, 1980, 301p.

2. Victim Services Agency, *The Experiences of Women with Services for Abused Spouses in New York City.* New York: 1982, 138p.

3. U.S. Law Enforcement Assistance Administration, *The Report from the Conference on Intervention Programs for Men Who Batter.* Washington, D.C.: U.S. Government Printing Office, 1981, 47p., app.

4. Edna T. Walker, *Family Trouble Clinic: a Police-Social Work Approach to Family Violence.* Detroit: Family Service of Detroit and Wayne County, 1979, 45p., app.

CHAPTER 19

CRIMES AGAINST
THE ELDERLY

A survey of crimes against the elderly in 26 cities across the United States showed that this group has the lowest aggregate rate of victimization. Furthermore, they have the lowest rate of victimization for every personal crime except larceny with contact (purse-snatching and pocket-picking), for which they have the highest rate of any age group. Most personal victimization of the elderly includes theft. Violence without theft accounted for only 17 percent of crimes against the elderly in this nationwide survey. The elderly were least likely to be either attacked or injured, and serious injury was rare. The elderly were not likely to protect themselves; even the least aggressive forms of self-protection, such as screaming or calling for help, were rarely used. Crimes against the elderly were more likely than those against younger persons to be reported to police. Almost one-half of all victimizations of the elderly were brought to police attention.[1]

Somewhat different findings were obtained from a study of responses by elderly crime victims during and after victimization. Data from the 1976 National Crime Survey showed that over 50 percent of a sample of victims 60 years of age and older used some method of self-defense when confronted with the offender. About 25 percent screamed or tried to run away, 10 percent tried to use force or branish a weapon, and 10 percent tried to reason with the offender. Victims who tried to reason with the offender were more likely to escape without injury than those who used force.[2]

While the elderly are the least victimized of all age groups, they have the highest fear of crime and are more likely to change their behaviors and lifestyles because of their fears. One study found that the anxieties of elderly persons in urban areas impose restrictions on their lifestyles and evoke feelings of depression and loneliness. Fear of street crime was especially strong, and harassment by teenagers was the type of victimization reported most frequently.[3]

When victimized, the elderly suffer more severely than other age groups because of their greater economic, psychological, and physical vulnerability. A University of Tennessee study found that the fear of crime among those who have been victimized severely handicapped the lifestyles of 84 percent of elderly victims.[4]

Seven demonstration projects of the National Council of Senior Citizens are among the most comprehensive attempts to reduce victimization of the elderly. These projects, begun in 1977, aimed at preventing crime against the elderly and assisting elderly crime victims in Chicago, New York (two projects), New Orleans, Los Angeles, Milwaukee, and Washington, D.C. All projects focused on selected neighborhoods with high crime rates and high concentrations of senior citizens, except Chicago, which adopted a city-wide approach. Although the seven projects pursued similar objectives, their emphases were quite varied. Some concentrated on victim assistance, others on expanded public awareness of the problen and ways to fight it. Other projects, such as those in Chicago and New Orleans, disseminated crime prevention information to groups of senior citizens, or stressed neighborhood strengthening activities, as in Milwaukee and Washington, D.C. The District of Columbia project established a successful escort service for seniors, while the Milwaukee project helped citizens form block clubs and implemented a comprehensive home security program for senior citizens.

Process and impact evaluations of the seven projects indicated moderate success in victim assistance, crime prevention, and public relations activities. Success in reaching large numbers of clients was tied most directly to the efficiency of its victim referral process, and projects varied greatly in this respect. A majority of the elderly residents surveyed said they received some crime prevention information during the project period, and almost half said it affected their behavior, usually by making them more cautious. Neighborhood-strengthening efforts were the projects' most ambitious and also their least successful activities. The ability of people to work together to combat crime apparently did not improve.[5]

Another evaluation of the same program showed that the elderly were generally interested in and receptive to crime prevention information and prepared to change their behavior as a result. Television was found to be the best way to disseminate public information about crime prevention. The most encouraging finding was that the programs that

138

were most organized and best planned were able to make an impact on their communities. Less organized programs had little effect.[6]

Based on these demonstration projects, the National Council of Senior Citizens has developed recommendations for planning and implementing crime prevention and victim assistance programs for the elderly,[7] a guide to training materials,[8] and a text for a training course on effective responses to the crime problems of older Americans.[9]

Only a few cities have established special police units to combat crime against the elderly, the largest of which is New York. The immediate effect of increased police presence in that city, which relied on intensive investigation and the liberal use of decoys, was encouraging: the number of robberies in which the victim was aged 60 or older declined 30.6 percent over the first seven months of 1977. The decoy technique, also known as "grandpop patrol", consists of volunteer police officers disguised as elderly men. Working with a backup team of detectives who pinpoint pattern locations, areas, times of day, and methods of operation, the "grandpop" squad acts to reduce attacks on the elderly.

Other cities, even those with special units, do not approach the level of effort in New York. For example, the Baton Rouge Police Department has a special Crime Against the Elderly Unit, but the squad focuses on crime prevention rather than on special investigative and decoy teams. Other police departments with units stressing crime prevention are Detroit, Rochester, and Maricopa County, Arizona.[10]

Many police departments have established crime prevention education programs for the elderly. The Waterford, New York, Police Department has established a senior citizen crime prevention program which consists of lectures and films teaching people how to carry pocketbooks and wallets, not to let strangers into the home without credentials, not to flash money when cashing monthly checks, and to try to be with a companion when out on the street.[11] The Stockton, California, Police Department provides eight weeks of classroom training in such areas as self-protection, consumer fraud, the use of mace, and the neighborhood watch program.[12]

Cuyahoga County, Ohio, has operated a Senior Safety and Security Program to help educate the elderly about crime prevention. The staff contacts all senior citizen clubs and organizations, nutrition centers, and large apartment buildings in six areas of the county with large concentrations of elderly residents. A sequence of nine presentations is given at each site, including a discussion of crime problems, a demonstration of locks, slide shows, and a quiz about crime.[13]

In a major study of crime prevention for the elderly in New York City the Nova Institute found that, while the elderly are less likely to be victims of most kinds of crime, they are disproportionately the victims of some kinds, including robbery and grand larceny when the victim was present and force was used. Programs designed to protect the elderly typically involved personal escort and transportation, home security devices, communication and signal systems, and relocation services.

The Nova Institute concluded that escort services and court monitoring have proven ineffective in reducing crimes against the elderly, and that relocation of the elderly out of deteriorated neighborhoods is one of the best ways to avoid their victimization. For those who choose to stay in these neighborhoods, better home security devices such as good locks, door bars, and window gates, as well as buzzer systems that enable them to call for help from a neighbor, have been shown to be effective.[14]

A successful, comprehensive program for senior citizens is reported by the Walter P. Reuther Senior Centers in Detroit, Michigan. The purpose of this project was to mobilize senior citizens to become involved in crime prevention in their neighborhoods and to reduce the fear of crime. Crime prevention activities were organized at each of the agency's three senior centers, and funding and technical assistance was provided to six community-based organizations as subcontractors. Activities included escort programs, neighborhood and apartment watch programs, replacement of obsolete security devices, and development of bilingual crime prevention materials. Surveys conducted at the start and at the end of the project showed that senior citizens participating in the project experienced a reduction in victimization from 45 percent to 11 percent and a reduction in fear of crime from 75 to 62 percent.[15]

A valuable resource on crime prevention for the elderly is the American Association of Retired Persons. Their crime prevention unit has conducted research, published a variety of materials, trained police in the needs and fears of the elderly regarding crime, and initiated prevention programs using senior citizen volunteers nationwide. One of their chapters was the driving force behind the unique citizen-run volunteer police department in Sun City (Maricopa County), Arizona.

FOOTNOTES

1. U.S. Justice Statistics Bureau, *Crime Against the Elderly in 26 Cities,* by Ellen Hochstedler. Washington, D.C.: U.S. Government Printing Office, 1981, 36p.

2. Mary C. Sengstock and Jersey Liang, *Responses of the Elderly to Criminal Victimization.* Detroit, Mich.: Wayne State University, 1979, 16p.

3. University City Science Center, *Police Service Delivery to the Elderly.* Philadelphia, Pa.: 1980, 166p.

4. University of Tennessee at Chattanooga, *Crime and the Senior Citizen: A Victimization Study of the Elderly in Chattanooga.* Chattanooga: 1978, 46p.

5. National Council of Senior Citizens, Inc., *Criminal Justice and the Elderly.* Washington, D.C.: 1979, 4v.

6. George F. Bishop and others, *An Impact Evaluation of the National Elderly Victimization Prevention and Assistance Program.* Cincinnati: University of Cincinnati, Behavioral Sciences Laboratory, 1979, 233p., app.

7. *Supra* note 5.

8. National Council of Senior Citizens, *Criminal Justice and the Elderly: Guide to Training Materials in Crime Prevention and Victim Assistance for the Elderly* (2nd ed.) Washington, D.C.: 1979, 38p.

9. National Council of Senior Citizens, *Effective Responses to the Crime Problem of Older Americans,* Washington, D.C.: 1982.

10. Bernard Edelman, "The Blue and the Grey: Should Police Set Up Special Units to Protect the Elderly?" *Police Magazine,* 5(5): 57-64, 1982.

11. Harry G. Fox, "Senior Citizens," *Law and Order,* 26(6): 20-86, 1978.

12. Dennis Kelly, "Stockton Police Department's Senior Citizens Assistance Program," *Crime Prevention Review,* 6(3): 16-20, 1979.

13. Phil Jones, *A Report on Services to the Elderly: Cuyahoga County's Senior Safety and Security Program.* Washington, D.C.: National Association of Counties Research Foundation Aging Program, 1977, 13p.

14. Nova Institute, *Reducing the Impact of Crime Against the Elderly.* New York: 1977, 38p.

15. U.S. Law Enforcement Assistance Administration, Crime Prevention Project—Final Report, by W.G. Yagerlener. Washington, D.C.: U.S. Government Printing Office, 1980, 175p.

CHAPTER 20

EMPLOYEE THEFT

The president of a large firm decided that the company needed a photograph of its workers leaving after a hard day's work. The gates, normally left open, were closed and photographers were posted in a watchman's tower. The employees, who had not been informed of what was to happen, massed at the gates, the gates were opened, and the cameras clicked. As the workers started home, they left behind on the ground by the gate over 4,000 items — tools, parts, soap, towels, scrap, and a fifteen-pound sledge hammer.[1]

Employee theft presents a paradox. On the one hand, a great deal of it apparently does take place. In aggregate dollar volume it may be one of the most serious forms of crime in the United States. It is more costly than burglary, robbery, and other offenses that are so prevalent in crime statistics and newspaper headlines. Employee theft is prevasive, probably in all industrial sectors, yet no one really knows how much employees steal. Criminologists, police, management, union leaders, and shareholders for the most part are unwilling to admit that the problem exists at all.

There are two important reasons why the problem should not be ignored. First, in most cases, the costs of employee theft are born not by the employer but by society at large. Companies that do not do what they can to minimize internal theft will shift its costs to customers and taxpayers. Second, as the economy moves more toward service industries and as technology becomes more sophisticated, the opportunities for employees to commit serious crimes are likely to increase dramatically.[2]

Estimates of loss due to employee theft are so varied that Dwight Merriam believes them to be entirely indefensible. Losses are often expressed as part of inventory shrinkage, which is the difference between actual and book inventory, usually expressed as a percentage of sales. The National Retail Merchant's Association is able to report shrinkage by departments for retail stores, with 2 percent being the most frequently suggested and probably the most reasonable. Sixteen estimates of employee theft as a percentage of inventory shrinkage range from 30 to 85 percent. A shrinkage of 2 percent in absolute terms does not appear to be excessive, but average net profit in department stores is only 1.5 to 2.5 percent. Elimination of employee theft thus could increase profit and dividends by 50 percent. If employee theft is assumed to be 60 percent of a 2 percent shrinkage, and if it could be reduced to half its present level, a business with 2 percent profit on sales would have increases in profit equivalent to a large increment in sales.[3]

In one of the most important recent studies of employee theft more than 9,000 employees of 47 businesses in Minneapolis, St. Paul, Cleveland, and Dallas-Fort Worth anonymously provided information on personal and occupational characteristics, job satisfaction, perceptions of theft deterrents, and their personal involvement in a broad range of deviant workplace activities, including theft. Interviews also were conducted with 247 executives who provided information about a variety of managerial practices regarding employee theft.

In retail stores, the deviant activity most often reported was the unauthorized use of the employee discount privilege. Twenty-nine percent of respondents reported that they had misused this fringe benefit during the past year, 14 percent of them admitting at least monthly abuse. Other types of theft, such as taking store merchandise or money, were also reported. Seven percent of respondents revealed that they had taken merchandise, and 3 percent said they had taken cash from the company. In hospitals, taking medical supplies from the ward was the most frequently reported kind of theft, involving 27 percent of all employees. Some 14 percent of manufacturing employees reported taking raw materials or components during the year, 4 percent on a monthly or more frequent basis. Other activities reported included the theft of tools or equipment and the theft of finished products.

There also were consistent patterns of counterproductive employee behavior, such as taking excessively long coffee breaks and lunches, use of sick leave for reasons other than illness, and use of alcohol and drugs at work. Those employees who reported above average theft were more likely to indicate above average participation in these other kinds of deviance.

In all three types of industry, younger and single employees reported the highest levels of property theft or misuse. In each industry those employees with the most unrestricted access to and knowledge about the property stolen were also more likely to steal. In addition, more dissatisfied employees were more often involved in theft and other deviant behavior.

Analysis of security operations indicated that preventing employee theft was not given top priority. Those organizations with clearly defined theft-control policies, those in which theft control had been incorporated into the inventory control system, and those that used pre-employment screening for prospective employees had lower levels of employee theft. It was also found that the higher the proportion of employees apprehended, the lower the theft rate. In general, the results of the study suggested that employee theft can be prevented only through a conspicuous and consistent climate of control of internal theft at all occupational levels.[4]

Several textbooks, manuals, and articles in professional journals have recently been published on the prevention of employee theft. Carson argues that employee honesty must be managed and supervised in the same way as competence and performance. Requiring employee accountability will reinforce honesty, reduce the temptation to steal, cut loses to internal theft, improve employer-employee relations, and increase profits. Carson outlines a step-by-step procedure that can be used by any business to encourage employee honesty.[5] Curtis maintains that employee honesty is often a reflection of the attitudes and actions of management. Management style will determine the extent to which most company employees will remain honest.[6]

In retail industries the cost of employee pilferage exceeds the cost of shoplifting. An internal control program proposed in an article in *Security Management* involves careful management of all employees, including sales, security, and maintenance personnel.[7] Effective internal control is said to depend on interdependence of employees, separation of responsibility, immediate indication of loss by management, supervised record-keeping, limited exposure of merchandise, random record processing, control of precedures, enforceability of employee duties, and critical-point audits. In addition, security devices can hinder the possibility of internal losses. These include central alarms, key control, locks and safes, isolated employee parking areas, stockrooms, patrol of high-value items, designated entrances and exits, safe storage of employee coats and packages, identifying name badges, briefcase inspection, two-way mirrors, vents, catwalks, electronic sensing devices, adequate lighting, and professional security personnel.[8]

An entirely different approach is proposed by Perryman, who argues that such high-security methods and aggressive policing of applicants and workers may be counterproductive. Any program that casts suspicion on employees, in Perryman's view, is likely to foster negative feelings that may be translated into greater alienation, declining motivation, and overall decreases in the level of job satisfaction. Perryman concludes from his studies that the outcome may be even greater tendencies toward internal theft. Instead, altering the work setting to reduce alienation and increase motivation and satisfaction may yield the desired results.[9]

Merriam examines four different ways of controlling and reducing employee dishonesty: screening applicants; procedures and devices to make theft more difficult or apprehension easier; improving job satisfaction; and apprehension and prosecution. All four clusters of strategies offer some means of reducing internal theft, but in practice the control of theft is *ad hoc* and inefficient. Needed is a balance of screening techniques, procedures to reduce opportunity, effective management, and apprehension and sanctioning processes. Theft control must be balanced against the employee's right to a personally and professionally productive occupation.

Donald Newman proposes that employers restructure the work experience to create new opportunities for job satisfaction. A first step is profit-sharing, which gives employees an economic interest in company success and rewards them individually for their collective efforts. Employees of one large retailer receive $20,000 to $50,000 when they retire; inventory shrinkage is less than 1 percent. Increasing job satisfaction is a most desirable strategy in controlling theft because several causes of theft are addressed and the needs of employees are recognized.[10]

FOOTNOTES

1. Sheryl Leininger (ed.), *Internal Theft Investigation and Control.* Los Angeles: Security World, 1975, 102p.

2. Richard F. Sparks, "The Paradox of Employee Theft: a Delimma for Management," *New Jersey Bell Journal,* 5(2): 18-27, 1982.

3. Dwight H. Merriam, "Employee Theft," *Criminal Justice Abstracts,* 9(3), 380p.

4. University of Minnesota, Sociology Department, *Theft by Employees in Work Organizations,* by John P. Clark and Richard C. Hollinger. Minneapolis: 1981, 278p.

5. Charles R. Carson, *Managing Employee Honesty: A Systematic Approach to Accountability.* Los Angeles: Security World, 1977, 230p.

6. Bob Curtis, *How to Keep Your Employees Honest.* New York: Lebhar-Friedman Books, 1979, 229p.

7. David L. Steeno, "Retail Security Tackles the Internal Threat," *Security Management,* 22(10): 14-20, 1978.

8. *Ibid.*

9. M. Ray Perryman, "A Neglected Institutional Feature of the Labor Sector of the U.S. Economy," *Journal of Economic Issues,* 15(2): 387-395, 1981.

10. *Supra* note 3, pp. 397-406.

CHAPTER 21

CRIME IN MASS TRANSIT SYSTEMS

Studies of mass transit crime in major American cities, including New York, Philadelphia, Chicago, and Newark, N.J., have found crime and the fear of crime to be significant and increasing problems in most conventional mass transportation systems. The results include not only passenger injury or loss and damage to transit property, but also loss in revenue from fearful citizens no longer using the transit system.

During a single month the New York transit system experienced 558 reported robberies, 982 larcenies, and 57 assaults. In the first eight months of 1980, 15 murders were committed on subways, up to 50 percent from the previous year. In 1977 the Chicago transit system reported 1,638 incidents of larceny; Boston, 147 cases of aggravated assault: Los Angeles, 18.250 violations of drug laws; and Milwaukee, 5,400 cases of vandalism against transit property.[1]

In response, several cities (New York, Chicago, Boston, Philadelphia) have expanded their patrol forces. San Francisco and Washington, D.C., two cities where new systems have opened in recent years, are experimenting with innovative policing operations. Transit police in these cities have modern communications systems, work in teams of two or more officers, and are encouraged to join undercover units. Several studies have found it difficult to tell how effective various approaches are in dealing with transit crime because of differences in station design, passenger characteristics, and the crime-fighting strategies and resources of transit police in different jurisdictions. New York's labyrinth of subterranean passageways and pillars, for instance, makes electronic surveillance impossible, yet this is an effective tool on the open and unobstructed platforms of Chicago.[2]

Other methods include the use of police dogs, randomized police patrol schedules, closed-circuit television, alarms, exact-fare boxes, improved lighting, and architectural changes. These methods appear to have had varying degrees of success in different transit systems, but evaluation has been complicated by such problems as regional differences in defining, recording, and reporting crimes.[3]

Findings of a study of mass transit crime and a plan for its prevention are offered by the Citizens Crime Commission in Philadelphia, where over 100 million passengers a year ride the subways. Mass transit crime in Philadelphia during 1980 included five murders, one rape, 481 robberies, 198 aggravated assaults, seven burglaries, and 21 larcenies. A total of 171 simple assaults, 302 incidents of vandalism, 14 incidents involving graffiti, 104 fare evasions, 51 trespassing offenses, 218 rowdy behavior offenses, and 131 other miscellaneous offenses also were reported. Of all major crimes in the city in 1980 (713 were reported), 57.5 percent were committed in the subway system.

The risk of victimization in the subway was highest in the late evening and early morning. Passengers correctly perceived that it was safer during rush hours than in off-peak hours. Among all the mass transit system's crime prevention methods, passengers preferred the presence of uniformed officers on the subway platforms and in the cars.

The prevention strategy developed by the Citizens Crime Commission of Philadelphia included the following: deployment of police patrol, surveillance of stations, security design of station environments, maintenance of stations and vehicles, prosecution of offenders, coordinated community crime prevention, data collection, and coordination of law enforcement efforts. Cost-effective measures for achieving these improvements include flexible patrol, targeting patrols in areas with high crime rates through a transit crime information system, coordinated control of one police force in University City, reward systems to improve police morale, use of above-ground patrols to check stations and surface vehicles, creation of a special court to process all transit offenses, and adoption of a restitution program for transit crime victims.[4]

A nationwide survey of policing mass transit systems determined that the crime problem is concentrated in the nation's largest cities, is of greater magnitude on rapid-rail than bus systems, and generally reflects the environment of surrounding communities. Passengers accurately perceive the extent and distribution of transit crime, and ridership patterns are influenced by perceptions of crime and security. Research on the effect of saturation patrol in rapid-rail systems has found that, although saturation patrol reduces crime, its effects diminish over time and there is some displacement to non-transit areas. Other policing activities have not yet been tested for their effects on transit crime.[5]

The American Society for Industrial Security holds that transit crime can be largely attributed to inadequate prevention and antiquated subway architecture. The Metrorail system in Washington, D.C., has the lowest crime rate in mass transit systems nationwide, in part because it is new and because it has architectural features ideally suited to crime prevention — unobstructed lines of observation; long, straight escalators; adequate lighting; closed circuit TV with monitors at each station; and recessed walls, difficult to mark with graffiti.

Increasing the number of transit police, in the opinion of the American Society for Industrial Security, is not the answer to the crime problem in transit systems. This group recommends better architectural design, sentences involving restitution to victims, community involvement in crime prevention, experimental projects designed to prevent graffiti, public information programs, and more cooperation between federal, state, and local law enforcement and judicial officials in handling mass transit crime.[6]

Procedures and plans for safe and secure transit stations are described in a five-part report by the U.S. Transportation Department. The report describes the criminal's perspective of transit crime as well as security from the passenger's perspective. A step-by-step procedure for planning counter-measures is outlined for use by transit planners.[7]

FOOTNOTES

1. American Society for Industrial Security, "Mass Transit Crime: Are the Animals Running the Farm?" *Security Management,* 25(1): 41-44, 1981.

2. Edward Kiersh, "Protecting the Commuter," *Police Magazine,* 3(5): 36-43, 1980.

3. Transportation Systems Center, *Proceedings* of a workshop on methodology for evaluating effectiveness of transit crime reduction

measures in automated transit systems. Cambridge, Mass.: 1977, 112p.

4. Citizens Crime Commission of Philadelphia, *A Strategic Response to Mass Transit Crime,* by Matthew Silverman. Philadelphia: 1981, 196p.

5. U.S. National Institute of Law Enforcement and Criminal Justice, *Policing Urban Mass Transit Systems: National Evaluation Program Phase I Report,* by L. Siegel and others. Washington, D.C.: 1979, 55p.

6. *Supra* note 1.

7. U.S. Transportation Department, *Planning Procedures for Improving Transit Station Security, Final Report,* by Larry G. Richards and Lester A. Hoel. Washington, D.C.: U.S. Government Printing Office, 1980, 62p.

CHAPTER 22

ORGANIZED CRIME

Until the 1970s most scholars and researchers, as well as the media and the public, believed that there was in the United States a conspiracy of a national crime syndicate. That syndicate was the Italian Mafia, an invisible, omnipotent government of the underworld. The political origins of the conspiracy theory can be traced to the Kefauver Committee hearings of 1950-51. The activities of that committee dominated the headlines during those years and swayed professional and popular opinion toward the notion that organized crime was controlled and administered by a nationwide conspiracy.

Scholars today do not support the Kefauver Committee's conclusion. Its work, they claim, was a study in miseducation, the strengthening of old myths that should have been laid to rest. Yet for a generation to come, its widely heralded reports provided material for college textbooks, journalistic accounts, and official studies, including the 1967 report of the President's Commission on Law Enforcement and Administration of Justice.

Without denying the existence of criminals of Italian ancestry with a strong sense of family kinship and a heritage of defying authority, students of organized crime now contend that there are no godfathers, that there is no Mafia behind an international or national network of organized crime. Our misconceptions and unsupported assumptions, in their view, have seriously misled us with respect to both what organized crime is and how to deal with it. Mafia families are traditional social systems organized by action and by cultural values that have nothing to do with bureaucratic virtues. Like all social systems, they have no structure apart from their functioning, nor do they have structure independent of their current personnel. The conspiracy theory, according to which gangsters of Italian descent dominate organized crime, fails to explain the proliferation of independent local and regional crime groups. The theory also fails to grasp the symbiotic relationships among professional criminals, customers, politicians, and businessmen in most organized crime activities.

The latest reports of the major organized crime commissions in the United States concur with the scholars. The commissions generally agree that the Mafia "godfather" does not exist. They document how, even in the last decade, other groups have organized their own criminal societies, repeating the pattern of earlier immigrants. The origins and nature of organized crime have thus undergone a profound reinterpretation in the 1970s.

Powerful social, economic, and political forces favor the existence of organized crime in the United States. Federal, state, and local governments, as well as innumerable citizens organizations, have not been able to eliminate organized crime. Most crime commission reports observe that organized crime will continue to flourish as long as there is a market for illegal goods and services. Many crime families are incapacitated through loss of members to murder by rival groups or to incarceration, yet the loan sharking, gambling, drug trafficking, and infiltration of legitimate business continues because of the enormous profits these activities bring. If organized crime rests on a firm foundation of public support and patronage, the prospects of eliminating it or reducing its power are dim.

Many crime commissions believe that public awareness and concern are the most valuable weapons against organized crime, and that efforts must be made to expose the dangers it presents to soceity.[1]

Keating and Kennedy distinguish between traditional and functional organized crime, suggesting that law enforcement must "out-organize" organized crime with emphasis on intelligence gathering, cooperation, and an effort to obtain laws permitting non-consensual eavesdropping.[2]

The failure of enforcement efforts against organized crime can be attributed in large part to ill-conceived policies representing symbolic responses to complicated problems. Perceiving organized crime as an alien conspiracy seeking to subvert the political economy has resulted in head-hunting strategy that does little to correct the real problem. Criminal organizations, like their legitimate counterparts, are able to regenerate, producing new enterpreneurs often more skillful and astute than their predecessors. This suggests that control of organized crime must focus on systems rather than individuals, for removing individuals leaves the system intact. Recognizing organized crime as subject to the pressures and constraints of its environment permits the use of strategies that alter illicit markets and reduce the capacity of criminal organizations to control them.[3]

What can and cannot be accomplished in a statewide effort to control organized crime is evident from a report of New Jersey's Organized Crime Task Force. That state's 1970 Criminal Justice Act and related statutes provided a combination of investigatory mechanisms that encouraged enforcement, and several major organized crime figures and public officials were prosecuted. Organized crime's hold on police began to loosen. Syndicated networks in gambling and narcotics distribution were disrupted and in some cases eliminated. Most important, business habits of organized crime had to change as the risks were heightened.

While much has been accomplished, the Task Force candidly acknowledged that the job is not done. Organized criminals have responded by altering their ways of doing business, becoming more sophisticated and less inclined to expose themselves to law enforcement scrutiny. Among the many Task Force proposals in the expanded use of civil remedies to allow the public to recover some of what it loses to organized crime.[4]

A recent *Guide to the Literature on Organized Crime,* covering the years 1967-81, presents references and abstracts of all major reports, studies, and articles on the topic and a comprehensive list of documents on the prevention of organized crime.[5]

FOOTNOTES

1. A history of the development of the conspiracy theory and its subsequent reinterpretation is presented in: Eugene Doleschal, Anne Newton, and William Hickey, *A Guide to the Literature on Organized Crime: an Annotated Bibliography Covering the Years 1967-81.* Hackensack, N.J.: National Council on Crime and Delinquency, 1981, 182p.

2. William F. Keating and John P. Kennedy, "New Thrusts in Organized Crime," *Police Chief,* 48(11): 26-28, 1981.

3. Clinton L. Pagano, "Organized Crime Control Efforts: a Critical Assessment of the Past Decade," *Police Chief,* 48(11): 20-25, 1981.

4. New Jersey, Organized Crime Task Force, *Report: 1978.* Trenton, N.J.: 1979, 76p.

5. *Supra* note 1.

CHAPTER 23

RAPE

According to the FBI's *Uniform Crime Reports,* in 1981 there were 81,540 rapes, attempted or completed, for a rate of 35.6 per 100,000 population.[1] Less than half of all rapes are reported to police: In 1979 reported rapes and rape attempts totaled 75,990, but the National Crime Survey estimates that there actually were 171,000 nationwide, 65,000 of which were completed. Of all rapes, the NCS calculates, 123,000 were committed by someone unknown to the victim.[2]

Much has been written on rape prevention, most of it addressed to what a woman can do to prevent becoming a victim through avoidance behavior, passive behavior when faced by a potential assailant, and aggressive behavior to counteract sexual assault. Some published materials examine possibilities for altering the environment to discourage rape or suggest social changes that might reduce its incidence.

One of the most comprehensive manuals on how to avoid rape is *Safe Within Yourself.*[3] This book argues that a woman can learn to avoid sexual assault or to disengage herself from an attacker without extensive training. Many of the self-defense techniques explained in the book require little skill or strength and can be learned through practice and training with another person. In particular, the book teaches women how to interpret and how to select the appropriate response. The advice is relevant to any assault, not only rape, since the topics examined include the nature and dynamics of assault, physical vulnerabilities of victim and attacker, physical defense techniques, weapons for defense, and methods of decreasing vulnerability to attack.

Over 700 agencies throughout the United States now provide prevention and treatment services for victims of sexual assault, and these should be used as a resource for rape prevention. A national directory of such centers is available from the U.S. National Center for Prevention and Control of Rape.

Produced to accompany the film entitled "This Film is About Rape," a British Columbia Police Commission rape prevention resource manual is also one of the better manuals available. It is intended to serve as a guide for service providers and resource people who disseminate information about rape prevention for both adults and children.[5]

There is general agreement on the correct proactive approach to reduce the incidence of rape. These precautions follow traditional target-hardening techniques: deadbolt locks and security alarms in residences; adequate lighting in yards, parking lots, and streets; and warning citizens about the dangers of unlocked cars, hitchhiking, and encounters with strangers. There is, however, great controversy regarding the reactive measures which should be employed in the event precautions fail and an attack occurs. Tactics to avert an assault are considered to be either aggressive or passive. Aggressive tactics (biting, kicking) are designed to frighten off the assialant. Passive techniques (crying, pleading) are intended to stall for time and to interrupt the offender's "fantasy trip" without increasing his level of anger. Some of these tactics will work sometimes, but no tactic will work every time. The method effective in any encounter is largely determined by the circumstances and interpersonal dynamics between victim and offender. Police officers specializing in rape prevention should share with the general population any information that may help women formulate their own tactical philosophy. Tindall points out that it is also necessary for law enforcement to "tell it like it is" on some aspects of rape that are not warmly received by the young female audience. For example: hitchhikers and scantily clad women are prime targets; some women send out conflicting signals and some men hear what they want to hear; and, if a woman knows the offender, passive tactics combined with no physical injuries are likely to jeopardize a court case.[6]

Of particular revelance to rape prevention are three studies on rape and rapists. Pauline Bart interviewed a sample of women who had been both rape victims and rape avoiders and examined the variables that distinguish the successful escape from a potential rape from the unsuccessful attempt to escape. She provides useful suggestions and recommendations for dealing with potential rape situations.[7]

Sussman and Bordwell, in *The Rapist File,* conducted a series of interviews with 15 rapists in state prisons to examine the psychology of rapists, particularly their motivation for the crime. The rapists' attitudes revealed that they considered a woman's body a "man's right" and that resistance justified force; few of the rapists expressed remorse or recognized their actions as criminal. The interviews showed that for the rapist it is the victim's struggle, and witnessing the pain and humiliation inflicted, especially during sodomy, that is most stimulating. The convicted rapists blamed deprived childhoods, pornography, and rejection by women for their behavior, and cited provocative female attire as evidence that their victims were "looking for it." Only one rapist suggested that his problem represented a failure to learn how to love.[8]

A final study with implications for rape prevention and escape from rape situations involved interviews with inmates who were asked how their victims might have avoided rape. A majority responded by saying that their victims might have avoided rape if they had talked to them and interacted with them as human beings, and if they had impressed on them the traumatic effects and aftermath of the rape.[9]

A long-range societal solution to the problem of rape is suggested by those who argue that rape represents a threat that can be used to keep women in a subordinate position. Potential as well as actual rape victims are suffering as a result of rape, and they are making lifestyle changes in order to avoid the dangers.

Many feminists charge that theoretical explanations of rape are reflected in the beliefs and work styles of rape crisis counselors. Individual rather than collective action to prevent rape is stressed by counselors interviewed in one study. Counselors saw little relationship between political and economic systems and the occurrence of rape, and they shied away from politics and those associated with it.[10]

Sanday undertook a cross-cultural study of rape to determine whether rape is inevitable as some have argued, or whether certain social processes allow rape to occur. Sanday's results clearly show that there are cross-cultural variations in the incidence of rape, and that there are identifiable differences between "rape-prone" and "rape-free" societies. Rape, in her view, is not a universal phenomenon, but emerges in societies characterized by violence and male dominance.[11]

A highly practical program of rape prevention for university women is reported from the Florida State University in Tallahassee. The University's Public Safety Department has developed a rape awareness program which includes presentations to campus residents, university classes, and other community and university groups. The presentations include a film that examines rape from the points of view of both the victim and rapist and a slide show that analyzes specific problems at the University, offers recommendations for rape prevention, and describes the justice system's response to rape victims. A rape prevention brochure, emergency telephone numbers, and posters are also part of the program. Community involvement has helped make the rape prevention program highly successful, and the numbers of reported rapes on campus have been low.[12]

The Portland, Oregon, Police Bureau provides self-defense workshops that instruct women on the value of assertiveness and teach them self-defense in a three-week, nine-hour workshop. In the first 18 months of the program 3,483 women participated in the workshops; 104 women who registered for the March 1981 workshop participated in a pre- and post-workshop attitude survey. The number of women who reported feeling "somewhat" or "very" confident in their ability to defend themselves from an attacker increased from 56 to 96 percent six months after attending the workshop, and 88 percent of the participants said that they had changed their behavior as a result. About half indicated that they would take action if someone touched or spoke to them offensively. Three women were victims of a crime subsequent to completing the course, and each was able to make use of skills and information taught in the workshops.[3]

FOOTNOTES

1. U.S. Federal Bureau of Investigation. *Uniform Crime Reports for the United States.* Washington, D.C.: U.S. Government Printing Office, 1982, 13p.

2. U.S. Justice Statistics Bureau, *Criminal Victimization in the United States, 1973-79 Trends.* Washington, D.C.: U.S. Government Printing Office, 1982, 61p.

3. Doris Kaufman and others, *Safe Within Yourself: a Woman's Guide to Rape Prevention and Self-Defense.* Alexandria, Va.: Visage Press, 1980, 114p.; Other valuable manuals are: James A. Smith, *Rapists Beware: a Practical Guide for Self-Defense for Women.* New York: Collier Books, 1978, 192p.; U.S. National Institute of Mental Health, *Rape and Older Women: a Guide to*

Prevention and Protection, by Linda J. Davis and Elaine M. Brody. Washington, D.C.: U.S. Government Printing Office, 1979, 171p.

4. U.S. National Center for the Prevention and Control of Rape, *National Directory: Rape Prevention and Treatment Resources.* Washington, D.C.: U.S. Government Printing Office, 1981, 150p.

5. British Columbia, Police Commission, *Rape Prevention: Resource Manual.* Vancouver, Canada: 1982, 89p.

6. Suzan Tindall, "Officer, What Should I Do If . . .?" *FBI Law Enforcement Bulletin,* 47(4): 2-7, 1978.

7. Arnie Cann and others (eds.), "Rape," *Journal of Social Issues,* 37(4): 1-157, 1981.

8. Les Sussman and Sall Bordwell, *The Rapist File.* New York: Chelsea House, 1981, 215p.

9. Hans J. Schneider, *The Victim in International Perspective: Papers and Essays Given at the Third International Symposium on Victimology, 1979 in Muenster, Westfalia.* New York: Walter de Gruyter, 1982, 513p.

10. Margaret L. Andersen and Claire Renzetti, "Rape Crisis Counseling and the Culture of Individualism," *Contemporary Crises,* 4(3): 323-339, 1980.

11. *Supra* note 7.

12. J.S. Sewell, "Rape Prevention Program at Florida State University," *Campus Law Enforcement Journal,* 11(3): 26-29, 1981.

13. Portland, Police Bureau, *Evaluation of the Womenstrength Self-Defense Program,* by Steve Beedle. Portland: 1982, 25p.

CHAPTER 24

ROBBERY

A total of 574,134 robberies were reported by the FBI's *Uniform Crime Reports* in 1981, for a rate of 250 per 100,000 population. Robberies comprised 4 percent of the total Crime Index of serious crimes and 43 percent of violent crimes. Considered a "bellweather" crime by many criminologists, robbery (which includes commercial robbery, muggings, and non-stranger robberies) is the crime most feared by citizens and most vigorously combatted by law enforcement.

Reported robberies rose 5 percent in volume over the previous year and 42 percent over 1977. The value of property stolen during robberies in 1981 was an estimated $382 million, with an average loss per incident of $665. However, the effect of this crime cannot be measured in dollars alone; it always involves force or the threat of force, and many victims suffer serious personal injury.

A majority of robberies reported in 1981 were perpetrated on streets or highways (52 percent of the total), followed by robberies of commercial establishments (13 percent) and robberies of residences (11 percent). The average loss in a street robbery was $441; bank robbery registered the highest average loss ($3,654), but comprised only 1.4 percent of all robberies. In 1981, 40 percent of all robberies reported were committed with firearms; 38 percent by strong-arm tactics; 13 percent with knives or cutting instruments; and 9 percent with other weapons.

Nationally, 24 percent of robberies reported in 1981 were cleared by arrest. Of those arrested 71 percent were under 25 years of age, 51 percent were under 21, and 29 percent were under 18. Seven out of 100 persons arrested were women; 60 percent of those arrested were black and 39 percent white.[1]

In contrast to the steady increases reported by the FBI, the National Crime Survey (NCS) conducted by the Census Bureau and published by the Bureau of Justice Statistics present a different picture of robbery trends from 1973-1979. NCS data do not include robberies of businesses such as commercial establishments, gas and service stations, convenience stores and banks, but personal robberies during 1973-1979 showed no general increase. The rate was 6.7 per 100,000 population aged 12 and over in 1973 and 6.3 in 1979. There were no significant trends in the rate of robberies with injury or without injury or in stranger robberies vs. non-stranger robberies.[2]

Many studies conducted during the past 15 years have implications for robbery prevention and control. For example, a study of armed robbery of convenience stores in Tallahassee, Florida, sought to test whether a store would be more vulnerable to armed robbery when (1) located on a street within two blocks of a transportation route, (2) located on a street with only a light amount of vehicle traffic, (3) located in a residential or vacant land use area, and (4) located in an area of fewer surrounding commercial activities. None of the four conditions was significant alone, but when considered together they all played a role. A convenience store was more vulnerable to armed robbery when it was located in a predominantly residential or vacant area near a major transportation route with little traffic on adjacent streets and little commercial activity.[3]

Findings from a study of bank robbers showed a marked change in the characteristics of robbers since the early 1960s. In 1964, in the Eastern District of New York, the robber was typically a white male in his late twenties or early thirties. He carefully planned his crime for maximum return and was caught only after lengthy and intensive investigation. He never worked with an addict or a woman. He was a professional criminal with a certain maturity and pride in his criminal activity and prestige among his peers.

The new breed of bank robber is generally black and in his early twenties. He is unsophisticated and there is little planning to his robberies. His associates are casually chosen, and women and drug users are sometimes admitted to the group. Contemporary bank robbers appear unaware of the odds, risks, and poor returns of bank robbery, as well as the enormous penalties. The FBI is able to identify and arrest 80 percent of the cases falling under its jurisdiction, an exceptionally high rate of clearance. Convictions also are high and penalties involve long prison sentences. This study suggests that the man in the street should be informed of the gap between the romanticized myth of the bank robber with his huge "hauls" and the realities of the crime with its small proceeds, high arrest rates, and long prison sentences.[4]

Another study looked at the relationship between the characteristics of banking offices and the number of robbery attempts they experience. This analysis suggested that both the type of neighborhood surrounding the bank and the presence of guards in-. fluence the risk of robbery in the expected directions. Banking offices in center-city locations run a relatively high risk of victimization, all other factors being equal. So, too, do banking offices located in ghetto areas, which suggests that bank robbery may be a local crime, at least in such areas. The most important means of reducing the risk of bank robbery was the presence of guards: In banks that normally would experience a number of robbery attempts in one year, the presence of guards could be expected to reduce that number by one. The list of bank characteristics that fail to register a significant impact, however, is surprisingly long.[5]

In a study of patterns of robber in Oakland, California, it was discovered that the variance of robbery within the city was very large: in a 3-year period in which the city's robbery rate was one of the highest in the United States, two-thirds of the half-block areas surveyed had no reported robberies at all. On the other hand, 25 percent of the robberies occurred in 4 percent of the half-block areas in the city and over 50 percent along 36 major streets. Most robbery apprehensions were the result of immediate action by citizens and police; detectives and follow-up investigations rarely played an important role. The two most intense areas of robbery in Oakland were skid-row late-hour bar and prostitution districts, and half of all robbery suspects were arrested either at the scene of the crime or in the immediate vicinity.

From the victim's point of view, resistance to robbery is likely to be more harmful than helpful. Victim interviews revealed that physical resistance — trying to hit the robber, struggle, or hold onto property — generally led to more injury. Yelling or screaming generally brought no adverse reaction and occasionally helped the situation. One-fourth of the adult and one-half of the juvenile robbers interviewed reported that someone had been hurt during their robberies.[6]

In a major effort to curb small-business robberies in New York City the Merchant Security Program subsidized the installation and maintenance of silent alarms, cameras, and warning signs in 523 small stores in 12 robbery-prone precincts in New York City. Participating merchants contributed, in most cases, about 25 precent of the cost of installation and rental of these devices over a 14-month period. An evaluation of the pilot program was conducted, and 250 of the 523 merchant subscribers to the program were interviewed, including all who had been victims of robbery. Victimization rates before and after equipment installation also were compared, as were rates of program participants and for nonparticipating merchants in the target area and in control areas of some similarity.

Findings of the evaluation did not show a clear reduction in robberies, burglaries, or larcenies in participant stores or target areas, but this was not taken to mean that the program had no effect on crime. Some precincts did show reductions in crimes against merchants, but the presence of other cirme prevention programs in the target areas obscured the reasons for this decline.

Participating merchants, however, viewed it as successful: 70 percent of survey respondents said they felt more secure in their stores because of the program, and over 28 percent said they also felt safer on their way to and from the store. The security devices apparently had a placebo effect: Businessmen felt they were doing something about crime and that they were receiving more individualized service from the police. Attitudes toward government and law enforcement also improved. Seventy percent of merchants interviewed said that their attitude toward the police was good, and 25 percent stated their attitude had improved as a result of participating in the program.[7]

An attempt to prevent armed robbery in the Nashville, Tennessee, area was judged less than successful. An alarm system established in 48 stores in two geographical areas for 6 and 12 months triggered an alarm directly to police cars and headquarters whenever "bait" money was removed from the cash drawer. On-scene apprehensions of armed robbers within target stores were greatly increased even though the system did not deter robbery, nor did it influence court disposition of the cases. The program did not deter crime, displace crime to other areas, or increase arrests in the immediate neighborhoods of the target stores or city-wide. The cost of prevention was greater than the savings associated with losses from robberies, but the program was continued because of a lack of any other means of arresting robbers.[8]

Recognizing that swift apprehension and positive suspect identification could help solve the problem of robberies, the Phoenix, Arizona, Police Department developed an experimental robbery reduction program. The strategy called for hidden cameras placed in selected businesses with a history of armed robberies, a squad of specially trained and equipped police officers, and statistical and analytical projections of the probability of robbery. The officers were released from all other duties and made available for the saturation of any areas where such crimes could be expected to occur. A month-by-month analysis of department reports for the first six months of the program, however, showed only that the rate of increase for robbery had been slowed.[9]

A system of "zero visibility patrol" was tried in Detroit which included a variety of well-known patrol techniques along with some unique features. A typical tour of duty would see the assigned police officers on foot patrol in teams of two or three. In appropriate cases the officers would work in disguise as decoys, accompanied by mobile patrols in unmarked patrol cars, taxi-cabs, delivery trucks, and similar vehicles.

The officers regarded the program as successful primarily because it increased arrests of robbers and other criminals. In 11 months of operation, the program produced over 800 felony prosecutions and over 300 misdemeanor arrests ranging from possession of unregistered guns to state traffic offenses. Six hundred and seventy guns were confiscated.[10]

A novel approach to robbery prevention for businesses, a variation of the system used in Nashville, has been tried by various police departments in the recent years. Robbery-prone businesses are equipped with concealed cameras that are activated when a "trip" bill is removed from the cash register. A clear picture of the robbery in progress makes it possible to identify the suspect and gain admissible evidence for trial.

In Seattle the concept was implemented using a rigorous experimental design, earning the National Institute of Law Enforcement and Criminal Justice's designation as an exemplary project. Robberies of business with hidden cameras were compared with those of a control group of similar sites without cameras, showing that the cameras effectively increased clearances, arrests, and convictions for commercial robbery. Fifty-five percent of robberies occurring in hidden-camera sites were cleared by arrest, compared with only 25 percent in the control group. Forty-eight percent of offenders involved in robberies at hidden-camera sites were convicted, compared with only 19 percent of offenders at control sites. Most important, commercial robbery rates decreased 38 percent from an 11-month period before the project was instituted to an 11-month period following project initiation. Non-commercial robberies increased 6.7 percent during the same period. In addition, in hidden-camera sites average time from arrest to disposition was about one month less than for control sites.[11]

The two documents most useful for planning robbery prevention strategies are the report of the Seattle project and a "prescriptive package" for police robbery control.[12] A step-by-step process for analyzing robbery patterns and developing action plans are detailed in these two documents.

Highly practical advice for the potential victim of violent crime is presented in an article by William Howard published in *Federal Probation*. The strategy that is most immediately effective, according to Howard, is psychological resistance; presenting oneself in an uncritical, non-threatening fashion will greatly reduce the likelihood of violence. The advice offered for avoiding victimization is as follows: avoid dangerous situations; dress and talk in a manner similar to residents of the neighborhood you are entering — that is, avoid the appearance of an outsider; walk firmly and with a sense of direction; avoid eye contact with loiterers on the street; avoid falling into a defensive fighting pose; if contact seems unavoidable, initiate the verbal exchange yourself, rather than letting the attacker do so; should escape be impossible, react to the criminal as a human being who, at this time and in this place, is capable of violent and dangerous behavior.[13]

Howard also constructed a crime prevention model for use by individuals with a high risk of being victimized — women, the elderly, immigrants, and lonely and depressed, and people of a habitually bullying nature. Such individuals should be taught to avoid situations conducive to victimizing behavior and, if they are caught in such a situation, to know which behaviors will make it psychologically more difficult for the criminal to behave violently. The basic assumption is that offenders are rarely sociopathic and, like anyone else, are restricted by the norms and ethical principles that determine socially acceptable behavior. He analyzes the interaction between the offender and his victim, which typically proceeds through five stages: avoiding dangerous situations, proper general comportment, conversation, short-circuiting a violent attack, and fighting back. Howard proposes practical steps the victim should take during each stage of the interaction.[14]

FOOTNOTES

1. U.S. Federal Bureau of Investigation, *Uniform Crime Reports for the United States, 1981.* Washington, D.C.: U.S. Government Printing Office, 1982, 15-18pp.

2. U.S. Justice Statistics Bureau, *Criminal Victimization in the United States, 1973-79 Trends.* Washington, D.C.: U.S. Government Printing Office, 1982, 18p.

3. Dennis C. Duffala, "Convenience Stores, Armed Robbery, and Physical Environmental Features," *American Behavioral Scientist,* 20(2): 227-246, 1976.

4. James F. Haran and John M. Martin, "The Imprisonment of Bank Robbers: the Issue of Deterrence," *Federal Probation,* 41(3): 27-30, 1977.

5. Timothy H. Hannan, "Bank Robberies and Bank Security Precautions," *Journal of Legal Studies,* 11(1): 83-92, 1982.

6. Floyd Feeney and Adrianne Weir, *The Prevention and Control of Robbery.* Davis, Calif.: University of California, Center on Administration of Criminal Justice, 1974, 87p.

7. New York City Police Department, *Evaluation of Merchant Security Program,* by Marvin Berkowitz. New York: 1975, 55p.

8. John F. Schnelle and others, "Program Evaluation Research: an Experimental Cost-Effectiveness Analysis of an Armed Robbery Intervention Program," *Journal of Applied Behavior Analysis,* 12(4): 615-623, 1979.

9. Patricia A. Lamson, "A Concentrated Robbery Reduction Program," *FBI Law Enforcement Bulletin,* 40(12): 16-20, 1971.

10. John F. Nichols and James D. Bannon, "STRESS: Zero Visibility Policing," *Police Chief,* 39(6): 32-36, 1972.

11. U.S. National Institute of Law Enforcement and Criminal Justice, *Focus on Robbery: the Hidden Cameras Project, Seattle, Washington,* by Debra Whitcomb. Washington, D.C.: U.S. Government Printing Office, 1979, 76p.

12. U.S. National Institute of Law Enforcement and Criminal Justice, *Prescriptive Package: Police Robbery Control Manual,* by Richard H. Ward and others. Washington, D.C.: U.S. Government Printing Office, 1975, 81p.

13. William B. Howard, "Dealing with the Violent Criminal: What to Do and Say," *Federal Probation,* 44(1): 13-18, 1980.

14. William B. Howard, "An Educational Aid for the Crime Prevention Officer: Some Social Psychological Strategies for Dealing with the Violent Criminal," *Crime Prevention Review,* 5(4): 25-34, 1978.

CHAPTER 25

RURAL CRIME

Although the crime rate in rural areas generally is lower than in urban or suburban areas, it has been increasing at a faster rate. In addition, some crimes are more frequent in rural areas, and these are subject to unique types of crime. During the 1970s agricultural crime — theft and vandalism of farm equipment, grain, livestock, lumber and pesticides — has increased 43 percent faster than crime in urban areas of the United States.[1] An Ohio study of rural crime reports that, although there were fewer reported incidents of violence, vandalism in rural Ohio was almost four times greater than that in urban areas.[2]

Rural theft and fencing rings have been particularly active in recent years. A study of professional theft and fencing of machinery and livestock in the rural Midwest discovered that homes there are burglarized with relative ease because of their remoteness and because of the trusting nature of rural people. Professionals often carry out livestock thefts with great ingenuity, concealing the fact or nature of the theft, and hiding the livestock in transit or passing it off as their own to stockyard dealers or fences. Victims are carefully chosen. Stolen animals are rapidly transported out of the community and sold. While most animals are taken when the opportunity arises, the thief knows at the time of the theft that he will be able to sell to a legitimate dealer who will not inspect animals or documents too closely.

Many of the same methods are applied to the theft of farm machinery. Professional thieves use counter-technologies to circumvent theft-proofing measures, and theft-proofing experts sometimes cooperate with thieves for profit. Market information is passed by word-of-mouth among thieves, fences, and customers. The fence does not reveal to the thief the identity of customers or the demand for a category of stolen goods, thereby preventing the latter from dealing directly with the customers. Most professional thieves maintain a respectable middle-class facade.[3]

Recommendations for preventing agricultural crime usually emphasize the speedy reporting of theft and vandalism, distinctive labeling of equipment and livestock, and better police training in agricultural crime.

No systematic evaluation of rural crime prevention is reported in the literature, with the exception of an overview of the first year of a project in six Minnesota counties, the purpose of which was to develop prevention strategies especially for rural areas. This project had six major objectives: to increase crime prevention efforts; to raise the awareness of county residents; to increase participation in crime prevention; to institutionalize prevention programs in local community groups; to test strategies suited for rural areas; and to define and analyze the rural crime problem.

The evaluation found that planning was subordinated to community action, which downplayed research and problem identification at both state and county levels. The one-year demonstration period was judged too short, but the project showed that highly motivated people who are willing to work part-time can be found in rural communities. Civilian crime prevention workers were more effective than those from law enforcement. It was therefore recommended that the project not be made part of an existing agency within the criminal justice system.[4]

A burglary prevention bureau in rural Monterey County, California, provides services such as Operation Identification, neighborhood watch, block meetings, a commercial burglary prevention program, school crime prevention information, shoplifting and armed robbery prevention presentations for merchants, consultation for builders and architects, and a speaker's bureau. Programs have been tailored to meet the needs of each of the county's three diverse populations: the co-op farming community, rural industry, and the ranching community.[5]

Resources available to the rural crime prevention worker include the National Rural Crime Prevention Center of the Ohio State University in Columbus and the Minnesota Crime Prevention Center in Minneapolis. A text on *Rural Law Enforcement*[6] and a manual on *Crime Prevention for Rural Environments*[7] are recent additions to the literature on rural crime prevention.

FOOTNOTES

1. Charles R. Swanson and Leonard Territo, "Agricultural Crime: its Extent, Prevention, and Control," *FBI Law Enforcement Bulletin,* 49(5): 8-12, 1980.

2. Dada Habibullah, *A Study of Selected Socioeconomic Variables Associated with Criminal Victimization in Rural Ohio.* Ann Arbor, Mich.: University Microfilms, 1979, 156p.

3. Rollin M. Barber, *The Professional Style of Rural Thieves and Their Vocabularies of Motive.* Ann Arbor, Mich.: Xerox University Microfilms, 1976, 127p.

4. Minnesota Crime Prevention Center, Inc., *Evaluation of the Rural Crime Prevention Demonstration Project,* by Glenn Silloway. Minneapolis: 1981, 52p., app.

5. Ron A. Qualls, "An Approach to Rural Crime Prevention," *Crime Prevention Review,* 5(1): 9-16, 1977.

6. Allen P. Bristow, *Rural Law Enforcement.* Boston: Allyn and Bacon, 1982, 202p.

7. Joseph F. Donnermeyer, *Crime Prevention for Rural Environments: a Systematic Approach.* Columbus, Ohio: Ohio State University, National Rural Crime Prevention Center, 1981, 25p., app.

CHAPTER 26

SHOPLIFTING

Of the more than seven million larcenies reported by the FBI in 1981, 11.4 percent were shoplifting offenses, representing an increase of 24 precent over 1977.[1] Based on a study of 27,198 arrests made primarily in Southern California during 1981, Commercial Service Systems, Inc., Reported that shoplifting losses continue to increase, confirming the FBI trends. Losses to supermarkets from shoplifting in the United States were estimated at more than $1 billion, and this does not take into account the costs of any countermeasures.

Male and female shoplifters in this survey were apprehended in approximately even numbers. Slightly more males than females were arrested in supermarkets (9.5 percent) and drug stores (4.9 percent). In discount stores, 7.3 percent more females than males were caught. Shoplifting is predominantly a crime of the young: 76 percent of those arrested in discount stores, 67.7 percent in drug stores, and 64.9 percent in supermarkets were under 30 years of age. The over-60 age group, which is increasing in size due to the general aging of the American population, made up only 2.1 to 6.9 percent of those caught. Those most frequently arrested were in the 18-29 age group. The next most frequently arrested were in the 12-17 age group.

An even distribution of arrests by day and by month showed that the shoplifter is always present in retail stores and that the retailer must apply counter-measures constantly. Arresting officers or agents report that shoplifters generally have enough money to pay for stolen items. This, plus the fact that half the supermarket cases involved one or more non-food items indicates that shoplifters are not desperate people stealing to feed their families. Limited funds may motivate a shoplifter to steal, but it seems a matter of priority what those limited funds will be used to buy.[2]

The National Coalition to Prevent Shoplifting also found teenagers to be the group most likely to commit this crime. In its study the average value of merchandise recovered from shoplifters was $8.69 in supermarkets, $9.56 in drug stores, and $48.46 in discount stores.

Ninety-one percent of the 100,671 students surveyed by the Coalition agreed that shoplifting is a crime; 70 percent felt that most shoplifters are never caught; 41 percent thought that stores force people to shoplift by charging high prices; and 65 percent felt that stores pass the costs of shoplifting on to consumers. Forty-nine percent of the sample admitted to having shoplifted at least once; 30 percent stated that they would continue to do so; 40 percent stole from stores in the past two years; 26 percent planned their crimes in advance; and 17 percent were caught. Of those caught, 46 percent were lectured by store personnel, 36 percent were detained, 40 percent were detained and their parents were contacted, 16 percent were arrested by police, 7 percent were taken to court, and 5 percent were sentenced or fined. Among the reasons cited by those who admitted to shoplifting were the following: They had no money to pay for the item (30 percent); they did it "for a thrill" (17 percent); they did it "on a dare" (11 percent); they acted on impulse (19 percent); and they "wanted to get even" (6 percent).

Of the 4,275 retailers surveyed by the Coalition, 77 percent acknowledged that they had a problem with shoplifting. Forty-three percent also reported a problem with employee theft. Of those retailers acknowledging employee theft or shoplifting, 74 percent felt that shoplifting was the more serious problem. The cost of shoplifting, averaged across 38 states and Puerto Rico, exceeded 6 percent of the total sales, but this figure included the cost of security and prosecution. Most retailers agreed that the costs of shoplifting are passed on to consumers and that the inconsistent and "soft" policies on prosecuting shoplifters were a problem.[3]

The National Coalition estimates that shoplifters cost Americans about $24 billion in 1980. This included the cost of security and prevention as well as the value of the merchandise stolen, which was estimated to be $3 billion (the estimate of Commercial Service Systems of over $1 billion included theft from supermarkets only).

Most experts divide shoplifters into three categories: the amateur, the professional, and the kleptomaniac with an uncontrollable impulse to steal. Lawrence Conner, executive director of Shoplifters Anonymous, a pretrial rehabilitation program in Pennsylvania, believes that there is a fourth type, the shoplifting addict. The kleptomaniac is the most rare type of shoplifter, and professionals account for only about 10 percent. The most common type of shoplifter is the amateur who steals on impulse for personal use. According to most studies, the greatest number are under age 21, with a peak age of about 15. In a Gallup survey conducted in October, 1979, 75 percent of the 13 to 18 year olds who admitted to shoplifting said they did it "for kicks." Most of the rest did it on a dare or on impulse. Excitement is often mentioned by shoplifters as a powerful motivation. George Furse, a psychotherapist, believes that hostility is a large part of shoplifting. Many shoplifters are expressing anger through stealing, either anger at the store for high prices or displaced anger from their personal problems. The modern discount store and the lenient treatment of shoplifters are often cited as having been largely responsible for the growth of shoplifting.

Prosecution is expensive and time-consuming, costing up to $350 per incident in employee time alone and taking up to six months. If there is no conviction, a retailer may face charges of false arrest. For these reasons, many retailers prefer to direct their efforts toward deterrence, and they spend over half of 1 percent of their sales revenue on security management, including electronic surveillance devices, employee training programs, public awareness campaigns, security personnel, and interior design strategies that minimize the opportunity to steal and facilitate surveillance. Closed-circuit television and electronic surveillance are among the anti-theft strategies that take advantage of modern electronics. Many retailers are also putting more money into training programs that teach both security and non-security employees how to protect merchandise and detect and respond to shoplifting.[4]

A study of shoplifting among 235 undergraduate students at the State University in Plattsburg, New York, showed that 53 percent had shoplifted at least once, 17 percent within the past two years. The majority stated that they would not turn in another customer they observed shoplifting. Ninety-three percent stated they would not want their children to shoplift, but only 9 percent thought it was wrong for others to shoplift. Fifty-six percent of respondents reported that two-way mirrors were effective deterrents. Other measures seen as effective were the presence of sales personnel, the positioning of guards at store doors, the use of closed-circuit television, the presence of signs threatening prosecution for shoplifting, and a familiarity with the store owner.[5]

Among the programs for preventing shoplifting reported in the literature is Shoplifters Anonymous, a non-profit agency that conducts classes using modern behavior approaches to turn shoplifters into honest customers, as an alternative to prosecution, and teaches prevention strategies to businesses faced with a shoplifting problem.[6]

The Placer County, California, Probation Department developed a shoplifting education program to acquaint adults and juveniles with the legal and financial consequences of a shoplifting offense and to inform shopkeepers about juvenile court procedures and the alternatives available when a juvenile is caught shoplifting. The program includes presentations to parent groups, service organizations, and schools; a slide show illustrating a typical shoplifting incident followed by arrest and court processing; and a publicity campaign using local newspapers. As more people became aware of the shoplifting problem and how to deal with it, the incidence of shoplifting as a part of the probation referral process declined from 20.5 percent to 12.9 percent after two years of program operation.[7]

Operation SOS, a shoplifting prevention program based on community involvement, was initiated in Fredericton, New Brunswick, Canada. The community was organized for joint action, involving several thousand junior-high, high-school, and university students, merchants, store employees and supervisors, shoppers, the mass media, and members of the criminal justice system. Data on both arrests and prosecutions showed that shoplifting declined during the year of the campaign. Arrests for shoplifting in Fredericton declined by 60 percent.[8]

From Nashville, Tennessee, comes a report of a shoplifting prevention program implemented in a convenience store. Aimed at students of a nearby elementary school, the program included visual instructions to students, tokens exchangeable for prizes for good behavior, visual feedback, and rewards for reducing merchandise loss. While the program was in effect, the incidence of shoplifting dropped from 32 to about 15 stolen items per week. When the program ended, this figure rose to 44. Since exact profit margins on each type of merchandise were unavailable, a precise cost analysis was not possible. However, assuming wholesale prices were marked up by a factor of two, the 58 percent decrease in stolen items during the program increased store profits an average of 42 percent.

The immediate rise in losses when the program was terminated suggests that it may be necessary to maintain such a program continuously. However, over a much longer period, its effects might be less dramatic.[9]

FOOTNOTES

1. U.S. Federal Bureau of Investigation, *Uniform Crime Reports for the United States, 1981.* Washington, D.C.: U.S. Government Printing Office, 1982, 26-29pp.

2. Commercial Service Systems, Inc., *19th Annual Report: Shoplifting in Supermarkets, Drug Stores, Discount Stores,* by Roger Griffin. Van Nuys, Calif.: 1982, 17p.

3. National Coalition to Prevent Shoplifting, *National Research Report on Shoplifting, 1980-81,* by Warren A. French. Atlanta, Ga.: 1981, 20p.

4. Jean Rosenblatt, "Shoplifting," *Editorial Research Reports,* 2(20): 879-892, 1981.

5. Robert J. Griffore and Douglas D. Samules, *College Students' Shoplifting: Incidence and Deterrents.* East Lansing, Mich.: Michigan State University, n.d., 10p.

6. Lawrence A. Conner, *The Shoplifters Are Coming.* Wilmington, Del.: Reports, Inc., 1980, 183p.

7. Art German, "An Entire County Combats Shoplifting," *Youth Authority Quarterly,* 31(2): 18-22, 1978.

8. Chok C. Hiew, "Prevention of Shoplifting: a Community Action Approach," Canadian Journal of Criminology, 23(1): 57-68, 1980.

9. M. Patrick McNees and others, "An Experimental Analysis of a Program to Reduce Retail Theft," *American Journal of Community Psychology,* 8(3): 379-385, 1980.

CHAPTER 27

VANDALISM

Nationwide, the most serious vandalism problem is found in the schools. Together with other types of school crime, vandalism has become a major problem in American schools and has affected the ability to educate. In the state of California alone property losses due to school vandalism approach $100 million a year.[1]

According to the latest studies, vandalism against schools is not simply a case of spur-of-the-moment, mindless destruction of property. Acts of vandalism against schools are typically carried out by young males acting in groups under circumstances that protect their anonymity and at the same time contribute to their sense of masculinity. Much school vandalism appears related to the student's need for peer approval. It may represent a repudiation of middle-class values or an attempt to cope with problems arising from sex role identification. Vandalism may also relate to the failure of the school to meet social, educational, or emotional needs of the students; his violence toward the school thus becomes vindictive.[2] Ernst Wenk has suggested that there are not only delinquent juveniles but delinquent schools.[3] In developing a policy for dealing with vandalism, administrators must consider the factors that lead to vindictive acts against the school.

A theoretical model of school vandalism distinguishes acts of hostility, acts of carelessness, and acts of thoughtlessness. All vandalism involves one or more of these three elements, and the particular element or combination of elements will suggest what countermeasures should be employed. Vandalism characterized by hostility may be reduced by standard security measures, positive peer pressure, and clearly stated and enforced consequences for engaging in such behavior. Vandalism characterized by carelessness may be reduced by incresing the potential vandal's feelings of identity with or "ownership" of the property. Vandalism characterized by thoughtlessness implies idleness and long periods of time without structured activity; increased recreational opportunities and carefully planned building design may reduce the incidence of such acts.[4]

Reducing school vandalism requires that students, faculty, administrators, and parents be involved in developing solutions. Guidelines for designing schools and setting up administrative programs for existing structures are provided in a volume entitled *Stopping School Property Damage.* This book also outlines design responses to the problems of accidental and non-malicious property damage and damage due to normal but hard-to-service wear and tear.[5]

A study in Los Angeles County compared a junior high school with the most vandalism with another school with the greatest reduction in vandalism. The entire faculty and a random sample of 100 students from each school were administered the adapted Goldman Pupil and Teacher Questionnaires. Compared with their counterparts in the low-damage school, students at the high-damage school had less positive attitudes toward their school, took less part in planning school programs, thought there were too few extracurricular programs, did not feel that school counselors were helpful, and did not cooperate or work to improve the school.

Teachers at the low-damage school considered outside students to be responsible for school damage, while teachers at the high-damage school thought students enrolled in that school were the vandals. Teachers at the high-damage school did not perceive their students as being respectful and did not accord the students respect. They seldom attended PTA meetings and few volunteered for extracurricular assignments. Students attending the high-damage school were viewed by their teachers as disloyal, lacking in school spirit, and unwilling to cooperate to make the school better.

To reduce vandalism, the study recommended providing mini-courses to cultivate positive attitudes and values, initiating good-citizenship assemblies, giving students and teachers more recognition to improve morale, allowing students more input to planning for school activities, and improving guidance and counseling.[6]

A finding repeatedly reported in the literature on vandalism is that vandals rarely attack property that appears to belong to someone who cares about it. This means that building design should clearly suggest individual, family, or community ownership and responsibility.[7]

The possibility of being caught in the act is said to be the best deterrent to vandalism, while good lighting and high police visibility are among the most effective means of keeping vandals away from school, parks, and other public areas. Another deterrent is good maintenance: broken equipment and evidence of former vandalism breed more of the same.[8]

A study of rural vandalism in Minnesota found that 80 percent of all acts of vandalism are limited to slight damage that can be described as childish pranks. Of those admitting to acts of vandalism, however, 20 percent reported having severely damaged or destroyed property. These more malicious acts are typically directed toward school property, motor vehicles, road signs, private residences and farms, and parks and playgrounds. Most rural vandalism involves individuals acting in groups. Supporting the group aspects of vandalism is the high consumption of alcohol and drugs. Most youths in this study engaged in acts of vandalism under cover of darkness and on weekends.[9]

In 1977 the U.S. Senate Subcommittee to Investigate Juvenile Delinquency called for a national effort to reduce school violence and vandalism. The Subcommittee recommended that school boards and state education agencies develop a program that includes community education, optional alternative education, alternatives to suspension, codes of rights and responsibilities, curriculum reform, police-school-community liaison, teacher education, training of school security personnel, counseling and guidance, carefully designed security systems, architectural and design techniques to reduce vulnerability, and student and parent involvement in vandalism reduction.[10]

FOOTNOTES

1. California Justice Department, School Safety Center, *Alternatives to Vandalism: Cooperation or Wreckreation.* Sacramento: 1981, 21p.

2. John P. Harlan and Charles P. McDowell, "Vindictive Vandalism and the Schools: Some Theoretical Considerations," *Journal of Police Science and Administration,* 8(4): 399-405, 1980.

3. Ernst A. Wenk, "School and Delinquency Prevention," *Crime and Delinquency Literature,* 6(2): 236-258, 1974.

4. Richard F. Thaw, *An Acts-Against-Property Model: A Case Study; An Extension of the Traditional Vandalism Model.* Ann Arbor, Mich.: University Microfilms, 1976, 191p.

5. John Zeisel, *Stopping School Property Damage: Design and Administative Guidelines to Reduce School Vandalism.* Arlington, Va.: American Association of School Administrators, 1976, 106p.

6. Marlene E. Harris, *The Relationship Between Student Attitudes and Vandalism in Urban Secondary Schools.* Ann Arbor, Mich.: Univeristy Microfilms, 1977, 196p.

7. Design Council, *Designing Against Vandalism.* New York: Van Nostrand Reinhold, 1980, 107p.

8. Clint Page, "Vandalism — It Happens Every Night," *Nation's Cities,* Sept. 1977, pp. 5-10.

9. Minnesota Crime Prevention Center, Inc., *Rural Youth Vandalism in Four Minnesota Counties.* Minneapolis: 1981, 49p., app.

10. U.S. Senate, Judiciary Committee, Subcommittee to Investigate Juvenile Delinquency, *Challenge for the Third Century: Education in a Safe Environment — Final Report on the Nature and Prevention of School Violence and Vandalism.* Washington, D.C.: U.S. Government Printig Office, 1977, 102p.

PART V

WHAT NEXT?

CHAPTER 28

SUMMING UP AND MOVING ON

Since President Lyndon B. Johnson's declaration of a War on Crime in the 1960s total national expenditures on law enforcement and criminal justice have increased dramatically. From 1971 to 1979 federal, state, and local expenditures for police, courts, and corrections have grown from $10.5 billion to $25.9 billion. Yet the national reported crime rate, with minor exceptions during certain years, has continued to rise. According to victim surveys conducted by the Census Bureau (which include unreported crimes as well), crime rates have remained essentially stable over at least the past eight years. Our crime prevention efforts, it seems clear, have not reduced crime at the national level.

In earlier chapters of this volume we saw that reductions in certain forms of crime in certain places are possible through such means as the installation of security devices and the involvement of citizens in crime prevention. While the national crime rate may remain unchanged, neighborhoods, communities, and individuls can reduce their own rates of victimization.

Still, the experiments and programs reviewed in this book make it abundantly clear that definitive answers to the question "what works" in crime prevention are hard to come by. With few (but very notable) exceptions, crime prevention programs have done little to reduce crime. This has been particularly true of efforts by law enforcement; for example, the Kansas City patrol experiments, the day-patrol component of the Nashville saturation patrol, the Nashville home-day-patrol component of the Nashville saturation patrol, the Nashville home-burglary saturation patrol, Kansas City's apprehension-oriented patrol, most Operation Identification programs, and the Minnesota Crime Watch. It has been true in delinquency prevention programs such as the Chicago Youth Development Project, the Chicago Area Project, and the Columbus, Ohio, school delinquency prevention project.

More successful in reducing crime in particular neighborhoods, or at least among participating homes or businesses, are those citizen-run programs that have active support and guidance of local police and those programs that are part of a more comprehensive, integrated effort to control crime. Such programs are even more successful in reducing fear of crime, in increasing citizens' feelings of control over their environment, and in improving the quality of life.

Many crime prevention efforts have potentially serious side-effects. One is high financial cost. For example, on completion of its experiment in saturation patrol the city of Nashville determined that, no matter how much crime was suppressed, permanent saturation patrol was too expensive. Another side-effect is an increase in citizen complaints about law enforcement, as occurred in the Kansas City apprehension-oriented patrol experiment. Conflict and discontent among police officers affected by crime prevention programs are another kind of cost. Two-thirds of the officers involved in the Wilmington split-force experiment, for instance, wanted the program discontinued. And finally, there is the displacement of crime to other places and times. Some crime prevention programs seem to do little more than move criminal activity around.

One hundred years ago Emile Durkheim, the "father" of modern criminology, theorized that crime is normal, necessary, and largely unpreventable, a conclusion confirmed by current studies. Durkheim implied that in a society with any degree of personal liberty, certain levels of crime are inevitable — the freedom of the criminal to pursue his aims is the same freedom that allows the genius to pursue his.[1]

Experience in totalitarian countries suggest that where personal liberty is tightly constrained crime rates still may be high. But Americans may be unwilling even to follow the successful path of democratic Japan, where respect for authority and individual deference to the group make crime prevention more readily achieved. Our preoccupation with individual freedoms and privacy, and our heterogenous population, make it unlikely that we will achieve a similar reduction in crime rates, at least on a national scale.

None of this, it should be stressed, means that attempts to prevent crime should be abandoned. Not only does citizen action to control crime have a salutary effect on the quality of life in any community, but measures to harden the target against crime are often effective for those who take them. By gradually widening the area of successfully protected

184

homes, businesses, and public spaces, we may achieve an impact that is community-wide, then go on to spread success to other regions.

FOR FURTHER HELP

Where can the citizen go to find help with a crime prevention problem or to volunteer his or her services in controlling crime? One obvious place to start is the local police department. Many departments have crime prevention officers on staff, and some have crime prevention units whose job it is to assist citizens with self-protection and anti-crime efforts. The city of Orange, New Jersey, for example, has several police-sponsored crime prevention programs, including Neighborhood Crime Watch. Over 40 civic organizations have participated in this program, with regular meetings held with the police department. The police also sponsor a volunteer citizen patrol, Operation Identification, and a block parent program. Numerous crime prevention publications are made available free to citizens, including manuals on organizing a block association, preventing robbery and burglary, and protecting against rape.

Most states operate crime prevention programs, and many have professional associations of crime prevention officers. In some states there are several governmental and private crime prevention agencies. The state of California, for example, has a Crime Prevention Center within the Attorney General's Office in Sacramento with 22 full-time employees. Its California Crime Watch is mandated to focus attention on local crime prevention programs, develop new and innovative programs, coordinate local crime prevention and public education efforts, and provide motivation and leadership to reduce crime by creating an informed public. The California Crime Prevention Center, a member of the National Crime Prevention Council, has produced many publications, films, and videotapes on crime prevention and provides training to both state and out-of state participants.

The California Governor's Office of Criminal Justice Planning works with the Crime Resistance Task Force to promote crime prevention programs involving law enforcement, citizens groups, local government workers, and businesses. The Crime Resistance Task Force and Office of Criminal Justice Planning have jointly developed a program of technical assistance, an important part of which is the Crime Prevention Exemplary Program. A recent document describes 35 exemplary programs, each of which has demonstrated superior achievement in reducing crime.[2] Government officials, criminal justice workers, crime prevention officers, and other community representatives may make arrangements to visit these programs for direct observation and technical assistance.

The California Exemplary Program is a means of identifying outstanding crime prevention programs throughout the state and verifying their achievements. The goal is to transfer technology and management techniques to other communities, thereby reducing start-up costs and allowing for adoption of proven concepts. For this reason, each program considered for exemplary status must agree to accept visitors.

Finally, the state of California has a Crime Prevention Officers Association whose 600 members propose legislation related to crime prevention, provide training, and disseminate information.

The National Crime Prevention Campaign, launched in 1978, works to reduce crime and fear of crime through citizen involvement and public education. The Crime Prevention Coalition, which helps conduct the campaign, includes the U.S. Army and Air Force, the Postal Service, the Boy Scouts, the AFL-CIO, the National Association for the Advancement of Colored Peoples, the National Education Association, the National Urban League, the American Association of Retired Persons, the American Retail Merchants Association, the National Council of La Raza, and 60 other national organizations. The diversity of the membership is evidence of a broad and responsive communications network of millions of Americans.

The contributions of public service advertising, education publications, and technical assistance are being drawn on by the National Crime Prevention Council. The Council provides leadership in capacity-building nationwide and works to increase communications between crime prevention programs and the sharing of resources, information, and technical assistance. Contact the National Crime Prevention Council at 805 15th Street, N.W., Washington, D.C. 20005.

A list of crime prevention offices throughout the United States and in foreign countries is contained in the *International Crime Prevention Directory,* available from: Brooks Russell, Director, Washington Crime Watch, Room 1455, Dexter Horton Building, Seattle, Washington 98104.

Pamphlets describing ways to protect property and person from various kinds of crime are available from McGruff, Box 6600, Rockville, Maryland 20850.

For abstracts of the literature on crime prevention, including such topics as arson prevention, auto theft prevention, residential security, contact the National Criminal Justice Reference Service at (301) 251-5500 or NCJRS, Reference Department, Box 6000, Rockville, Maryland 20850.

Finally, interested readers can consult the guides, manuals, and other publications on crime prevention listed in the next chapter.

It is a truism that the justice system, including the police, can only react to crime, not prevent it. Collectively, citizens play the greatest role in determining how much crime there will be. The evidence suggests there is much we can do to protect ourselves against crime. The first step is to get involved.

FOOTNOTES

1. Emile Durkheim, "Crime as a Normal Phenomenon," in Leon Radzinowicz and Marvin E. Wolfgang (eds.), *The Criminal in Society* (Vol. 1, *Crime and Justice*). New York: Basic Books, 1977, 657-661pp.

2. California, Crime Resistance Task Force, *Crime Prevention Exemplary Programs.* Sacramento: 1983, 82p.

FOR MORE INFORMATION

SELF AND HOME PROTECTION

Gerald S. Arenberg, *Protect Yourself: a National Manual of Crime Prevention.* Washington, D.C.: National Association of Chiefs of Police, 1980, 137p.

Judith Fein, *Are You a Target? A Guide to Self-Protection, Personal Safety, and Rape Prevention.* Belmont, Calif.: Wadsworth, 1981, 146p.

Gerald Hall, *How to Completely Secure Your Home.* Blue Ridge Summit, Pa.: Tab Books, 1978, 224p.

Warren J. Lucas, *Protection Made Easy.* Falls Church, Va.: C & L Publishing Co., 1981, 144p.

Robert McDermott and Theodore Irwin, *Stop, Thief: How to Safeguard and Secure Your Home and Business.* NY: MacMillian, 1978, 256p.

Hugh C. McDonald, *Survival.* New York: Ballantine Books, 1982, 177p.

Richard Rowe and Joyce Mallman, *Total Self-Protection: the Handbook of Crime Prevention.* New York, William Marrow, 1979, 286p.

U.S. National Institute of Law Enforcement and Criminal Justice, *Home Security, Book One: Basic Techniques of Home Guardianship* by James M. Edgar. Washington, D.C.: U.S. Govt. Printing Office, 1979, 18p.

COMMUNITY CRIME PREVENTION

ACTION and U.S. Law Enforcement Assistance Administration, *Urban Crime Prevention Program: Guideline Manual.* Washington, D.C.: U.S. Government Printing Office, 1980, 70p., app.

Georgette Bennett, *A Safe Place to Live,* prepared for the Insurance Information Institute and the Crime Prevention Coalition. New York: 1982, 136p.

Center for Community Change. *The Community's Stake in Crime Prevention: a Citizen's Action Guide.* Washington, D.C.: U.S. Government Printing Office, 1979, 44p.

Civic Action Institute, *Community Crime Prevention: a Neighborhood Action Guide.* Washington, D.C.: 1979, 20p.

Crime Stoppers-USA, Inc. *Crime Stoppers Operational Manual,* by Greg MacAleese and H. Coleman Tily. Albuquerque, N.M.: 1980, v.p.

Minnesota Crime Control Planning Board, *Block Club Organizing Handbook.* St. Paul, Minn.: 1981, 32p.

Minnesota Crime Prevention Center, *Planning Crime Prevention Programs,* by Marlys McPherson and Glenn Silloway. Minneapolis: 1980.

National Sheriffs' Association, *National Neighborhood Watch Program Manual: Guidelines and Suggestions for the Implementation of Local Neighborhood Watch Programs by Law Enforcement Agencies and Citizen Organizations.* Washington, D.C.: 1981, 38p.

U.S. Community Anti-Crime Programs Office, *Comprehensive Crime Prevention Program: Program Guide,* by Ruth Katz and others. Washington, D.C.: 1980.

U.S. Law Enforcement Assistance Administration, *We Can Prevent Crime.* Washington, D.C.: U.S. Government Printing Office, 1979.

U.S. National Institute of Justice, *Partnership for Neighborhood Crime Prevention.* by Judith D. Feins. Washington, D.C.: 1983, 66p.

U.S. National Criminal Justice Ref. Service, *Citizen Crime Prevention Tactics: a Literature Review and Selected Bibliography,* by J.T. Duncan. Washington, D.C.: U.S. Govt. Printing Office, 1980, 116p.

SECURITY MANAGEMENT

David L. Berger, *Industrial Security.* Los Angeles, Calif.: Security World, 1979, 361p.

Harvey Burstein, *Management of Hotel and Motel Security.* New York: Marcel Dekker, 1980, 200p.

Richard B. Cole, *Principles and Practice of Protection.* Springfield, Ill.: Charles C. Thomas, 1980, 414p.

Lawrence J. Fennelly (ed.), *Handbook of Loss Prevention and Crime Prevention.* Boston: Butterworths, 1982, 962p.

Gion Green, *Introduction to Security* (3rd ed.), Boston: Butterworth, 1981, 395p.

Richard J. Healy and Timothy J. Walsh, *Principles of Security Management.* Long Beach, Calif.: Professional Publications, 1981, 274p.

Charles F. Hemphill, *Modern Security Methods.* Englewood Cliffs, N.J. Prentice-Hall, 1979, 300p.

James E. Keogh, *The Small Business Security Handbook.* Englewood Cliffs, N.J.: Prentice-Hall, 1981, 258p.

Robert L. O'Block, *Security and Crime Prevention.* St. Louis, Mo.: C.V. Mosby, 1981, 452p.

Truett A. Ricks and others, *Principles of Security: an Introduction.* Cincinnati, Ohio: Anderson, 1981, 297p.

A. Lewis Russell, *Corporate and Industrial Security.* Houston: Gulf, 1980, 275p.

ENVIRONMENTAL DESIGN FOR CRIME PREVENTION

Oscar Newman, *Defensible Space: Crime Prevention through Environmental Design.* New York: Macmillian, 1972, 234p.

Oscar Newman, *Design Guidelines for Creating Defensible Space.* Washington, D.C.: National Institute of Law Enforcement and Criminal Justice, 1975, 213p.

U.S. National Institute of Justice, *Crime Prevention through Environmental Design. An Operational Handbook,* by Allan Wallis and Daniel Ford. Washington, D.C.: U.S. Govt. Printing Office, 1981, 232p.

U.S. National Institute of Law Enforcement and Criminal Justice, *Design for Safe Neighborhoods: the Environmental Security Planning and Design Process,* by Richard A. Gardiner. Washington, D.C.: U.S. Government Printing Office, 1978, 83p.

INDEX